RISE TO CON-QUER

RON + CAROL —
WE LOVE YOU! WE
WILL "CONQUER"
TOGETHER !!

RISE TO CONQUER

A call for Christian action

Larry Poland

CHRISTIAN HERALD BOOKS
Chappaqua, New York

Library of Congress Cataloging in Publication Data

Poland, Larry W
   Rise to conquer.

     1. Christian life—1960–   2. Christianity—
20th century.   3. Kingdom of God.   I. Title.
BV4501.2.P55547   248'.4   78-64843
ISBN 0-915684-48-9

First Edition
CHRISTIAN HERALD BOOKS, 40 Overlook Drive, Chappaqua, New York 10514
Printed in the United States of America

To Christian Mark,
    Desiree Marie,
    Cherish Faith, and
    Destiny Joy
with the hope that these children will rise to conquer

CONTENTS

INTRODUCTION

I was weary from traveling a continent as I boarded a flight from Mexico City to Los Angeles only to be jammed into a full airplane "six across." The two girls sitting next to me were returning from the International Women's Year Congress in Mexico City, Americans with decidedly Marxist convictions.

I say "girls," but the one was probably thirty-three, a journalist with a propensity for loud talk and authoritative proclamations on subjects about which she knew little. The girl traveling with her was about sixteen and given to hanging on to the journalist's every word.

I stayed out of the conversation for nearly two hours while trying to catch some much needed sleep. I gave up when the girls' conversation turned to Fidel Castro and his great strides in building a socialist state after having liberated the Cuban people. The sixteen year old announced loudly enough for me to hear that she was writing a love letter to Fidel (in Spanish) because she was "in love with his body." At *that* I broke silence.

"I hope you gals realize that I have stayed out of your conversation for nearly two hours," I said, "but when you say that you are writing a love letter to Fidel Castro because you are in love with his body, I think it is time for me to enter in!" They laughed, we got acquainted, and I began to probe a bit into some of the presuppositions on which the two, especially the journalist, were operating. It wasn't long before the journalist stopped our conversation, looked directly in my eyes and said, "Who are you anyway and what do you do.?"

Without batting an eyelash, I responded, "I am a plain-clothes agent in the Jesus Revolution, the only revolution that will ultimately be successful."

I couldn't have stunned them more if I had punched them in the nose. The entire nature of the dialogue changed as I presented the claims of this Jesus and his offer of free salvation and a share in his invincible kingdom.

I've been a Christian for nearly thirty years. I grew up in a Christian community of sorts. It was the home of what was then billed as "The World's Largest Bible Conference." It was the retirement home of the great American evangelist, Billy Sunday. The community is the center for two evangelical church denominations, a score of other Christian organizations, and a seminary. I grew up in a Christian home, always went to a Bible teaching church, and, as a teenage bellhop in the Bible conference hotels, carried the bags for and listened to most of the world's great evangelists and Bible teachers.

I attended what I consider to be one of the world's great Christian colleges, graduated from seminary, and entered Christian work despite my associations with the Christian community. I say "despite" because Christians were almost the undoing of my Christianity. I entered Christian service and puttered along in that a few years, keeping the rules, spouting the lingo, winning theological arguments, and earnestly serving my Master.

But if I had met those Marxist young women during those years of my life I would not have responded as I did to the question, "Who are you and what do you do?" I was a Christian worker. No more, no less, just a Christian worker. I hadn't discovered the KINGDOM.

Most of my Christian friends haven't discovered the kingdom either. Most of the Christians I meet in other countries haven't discovered the kingdom. The twentieth century church of Jesus Christ hasn't discovered the kingdom.

That's why I am writing this book, to proclaim to the church of our day the Good News of the Kingdom.

Christian, you had better fasten your seatbelt. What I am going to tell you will turn your world upside down. You are playing with fire, entering the big leagues, conspiring to overthrow, declaring war, dying to your former life, and entering the ranks of the kamikaze—all at once. If you act on this truth, you may soar like Jonathan Livingston Seagull, conquer like Alexander the Great, claim an inheritance that will make Howard Hughes' look like petty cash.

There is royal blood in your veins, nobility in your lineage, political power in your family, and you are destined to rule the world!

Read on.

1 Thy Kingdom Isn't Coming

In California, where I live, people communicate in strange ways, even by bumper sticker. One such communiqué read, "God isn't dead, I talked with him this morning." A friend of mine proclaims, "Not only is God not dead, he isn't even sick!" But it is a little preposterous to me to think that anyone needs to put a sign on an auto bumper proclaiming that God is not dead. That seems to me a little like proclaiming that water is not dry or the sun not cold.

It *would* be preposterous in some other ages or places but it is not so in this society, in this age. The church has probably done the most to write God's obituary for an onlooking world. It was a theologian, remember, that came up with the notion of the death of God. It was a theologian that came up with the bizarre concept of "Christian atheism." It has been members of the Christian community that have set forth the concept that we are in the "post-Christian era." And by "post-Christian" I do not refer to the idea that some societies have lost their first love and are languishing in a "post-Christian preoccupation" of some kind. This is both scriptural and obvious. But there are those proclaiming that the church is obsolete, Christian teaching is not relevant in a scientific age, and the new birth is a psychological phenomenon—that the *world* is post-Christian.

I admit that I am deeply sympathetic with those who make such proclamations, however. If a doctor were to determine a patient "alive," he would need confirming evidence from some vital indicators or life signs. To an

4

outsider I can understand why "death" would be the verdict on Christianity.

How many nations are being led in government policy, social reform, educational philosophy, or artistic pursuits by the teachings, philosophy, or ethic of Jesus?

Where in the 150 major nations of the world is the Christian spirit embodied in national life, international relationships, or even diplomatic verbiage?

Or take a look at those nations who claim a Christian root structure, heritage, or philosophical tradition. Are those countries leading the world in moral excellence? Certainly not the United States. I walked into a store in Nazareth, Jesus' home town, and observed America's *Playboy* magazine on sale. In my world travels I hear America described as a nation of wealth, power, and filth. People know. Our X-rated movies are playing in their theaters except where they have possessed more national conscience than we and banned them.

Popes Paul VI and John Paul II have taken some open stands on contemporary moral issues such as militarism and abortion, but outside of a handful of Protestant Christian leaders it is hard to find those that are making moral issues "Bible clear." If they are, they are often picked at from *within* the church as well as without as being too radical, too narrow-minded, or too puritanical. Legislators tell us, "We hear from the gays, we hear from the civil rights proponents, we hear from labor, we hear from management, we hear from everybody but the biblical Christians."

If the church fails to show life signs on the issue of direct involvement in the world, how is the church doing *internally*? Is it any healthier? I don't think so.

Too often the average local church is what Bob Harrington calls a "high steeple, no people" church. Its profile is post middle age and more concerned with social status and denominational matters than with the liberating power

of the Gospel. Its fare from the pulpit is on a par with
Rotary Club talks and its role as a redemptive agency for
troubled humanity is non-existent. This is obvious by the
lack of redemption of its members who, if their souls have
been redeemed, are fighting redemption of their lifestyles,
business ethics, moral standards and language.

The church is struggling unsuccessfully to maintain
consistency in its internal moral posture. Because of this its
impact on the global community is minimal. The present
missions force in the world from Protestant Christian
sources is between 50,000 and 55,000. Approximately sev-
enty percent of these come from North America and are
serving in a culture other than their own. But what are they
doing? Are they carrying the glorious goodness of personal
redemption to the masses of lost humanity? Are they proclaiming "whosoever believes in the Lord Jesus Christ will
be saved?" Are you kidding?

A survey of the activity of these missionaries indicates
that by *their own statement* less than a third (28 percent) are
involved in any way in either evangelism or church plant-
ing. From personal observation of the evangelistic effectiveness of the missionary in the field, I would personally
doubt if as many as 15,000 of the 55,000 missionaries are
directly involved in communicating to non-Christians the
message that answers the question, "What must I do to be
saved?" By this I mean they are not communicating the
clear message with sufficient effectiveness that a numeri-
cally significant number of unbelievers are placing trust in
Christ on an annual basis.

This is not to say that the missionary force isn't doing
a lot of really good things—in the areas of education,
medicine, agriculture and economic aid. The measure I am
using is the first dimension of Jesus' Great Command to
proclaim the Gospel and disciple those who respond. If that
test is put to modern missionary effort I repeat my question, "Are you kidding?"

Well, maybe the North American church is using its great wealth to underwrite the missions effort worldwide in lieu of actually transporting workers overseas. One thing that can be said is that on a relative measure of resources going into missions from North America as contrasted with that from other continents, we look quite good. In 1975 we gave $656 million dollars from North America to Protestant missions. In fact, giving to evangelical missions as reflected by the figures of the two major associations of evangelical missions indicates that giving is up 88.6 percent in the last three years!

A sign of life for the church? Hardly. Everyone knowledgeable in giving to Christian causes knows that even the practice of tithing (ten percent of income to the cause of Christ) is mythology, even in those denominations that make this a strong expectation of their membership. In the *highest* giving churches and denominations the ratio may run as high as three percent or maybe four percent. If the church even took tithing seriously, more money would be released than missions (with its present mediocre management) would be able to use wisely. Naturally the percentage of the one to two percent given to most churches that ever gets to the overseas missionary effort (to say nothing of the missions effort that is involved in direct proclamation of the Gospel) is kiddy allowance.

Some time ago I was being ushered by a pastor through his new church sanctuary. He was telling me how much the carpet cost per square yard, that the structure cost $800,000, and that their $125,000 pipe organ was on order. We walked through the sanctuary and into the hall which linked it with the educational building. In the hallway I noticed a bronze plaque which said, "OUR MISSIONARY."

I stopped the pastor and said, "You know, Pastor, with the resources that this church possesses, you could be supporting one hundred missionaries." He laughed heartily. The idea was ridiculous. The idea is obviously ridiculous to most American churches. This I find difficult to interpret as a sign of life.

Please do not interpret my comments as an effort to destroy or discredit the Church or the evangelical missions effort. The Church has accomplished a lot for Jesus Christ and the incredible victories of the modern missions movement are laudable. But what hurts me is the comparison of *what is being done* with *what could be done*, of actual accomplishment with what God says is our potential.

But I guess that raises the question, "If the Church of Jesus Christ *Militant* has become the church of Jesus Christ *Milquetoast*, why?

I personally feel that the cause can be traced to two chronic diseases. The first is the pollution of the Church. You may have thought it strange that I have been using a capital letter on the word church in some places and not in others. No error. The Church of Jesus Christ, the universal and mystical body of all true believers in Jesus, justifies a capital "C." If nothing else is clear from the teachings of Jesus, the human organization may overlap with the mystical body, but the two are not necessarily coterminous. False teachers and people who proclaim "Lord, Lord" inhabit the organization but are not part of the organism.

The Church (note the capital "C") is constituted only of the redeemed, those who have surrendered their human wills and whose faith in Jesus Christ is personal. The church (note the small "c") is a motley assortment of organizational entities made up of those who have identified in some way with Christendom whether or not they have ever been reborn into the Church.

And therein lies the problem. How can "the church of Jesus Christ" (note that small "c") ever take an aggressive stance against evil when evil is, in part, its stock in trade. How can an organization that cannot even come up with a common basis for authority, to say nothing of a biblical world view, proclaim to a spiritually lost world "thus saith the Lord?" If you asked three people in the church if the world was lost, they'd have four opinions.

When the basic requirements for entry into a "Christian" group are reduced to a simple acceptance by a jury of one's peers, you have reduced the *Church* to the *church* and you immobilize and paralyze it as an agent of change in a degenerate world system. It is dead.

The second chronic disease is equally debilitating. It is the decapitation of the reality that Jesus said we should pray for, that his kingdom would come. If every believer that had ever prayed "Thy kingdom come" had even the vaguest understanding of what the coming of the kingdom of Jesus Christ is all about, new life would instantly be infused into both the Church and the church. This concept is dynamite.

The coming of the kingdom of Jesus includes the following:

The return of the King, his second coming;

Every Christian's imminent accountability for his thought, behavior and motivation;

The rectification of all wrongs in and out of the *Church* and the *church*;

The judgment of all evil and especially evil *systems* (like nations and churches);

The dispensing of rewards to all members of the *Church*;

The inauguration of a new era of world control and divine influence in every area of human existence.

While the sequence and timing of the above are the subject of varied interpretations of scriptural teaching and discussion, these clearly *are* the implications.

If every believer, or even a significant proportion of believers, were minded to hasten the coming of the kingdom of Jesus Christ by praying for it, certainly something would change to resuscitate or resurrect the Church (if not the church). Christians absolutely *cannot* believe, in any more than the most superficial manner, that the kingdom of Jesus Christ is coming. If we did, we would have the entire fleet in readiness, as when a returning space capsule is going through re-entry. Our eyes would be fixed on the heavens and all Christians would be stationed and prepared.

But unless something dramatic happens to the body of Christ, the coming of the King will be chaos. Our fleet will be in mothballs and most of our personnel will be sitting in front of their big blue tubes being informally socialized into the value system of the enemy forces. The ragtag bunch of faithful on hand to greet Jesus won't overflow a rowboat.

We Christians had better do one of two things:

1) We had better hear Christ's call for action; or

2) We had better start praying, "Don't let thy kingdom come, we ain't ready!"

2 The World Returns to Its Folly

Remember the days when the cartoonists pictured fundamentalists with long hair, sandals, white robes and sandwich boards declaring, "Repent, the end of the world is nigh"? Those were the days when, amid blind optimism, the world ridiculed believers in Bible prophecy regarding the "end of the world." They expressed the foolishness of a poem I learned when I was a kid about the blind optimist:

> An optimist fell from a skyscraper,
> and, as he passed each window bar,
> he said with a smile to the people inside,
> "Things are all right so far!"

Things have changed. The optimistic world has gotten increasingly grim. In fact, about the only place you can go today to find hope is to those same ridiculed fundamentalists (or evangelicals, as most of them like to be called today) who are still preaching the end of the age and the second coming of Jesus Christ.

The "prophets of doom" are now on the six o'clock news, too. Dennis Braithewaite of Toronto laments, "The news today is just too awful to bear scrutiny." Walter Cronkite says, "Many times, I'd rather be a song-and-dance man bringing some levity to you instead of wrack and ruin. But we are on the threshold." Tom Alderman in *Canadian Magazine* observes that "massacres, fires, earthquakes, riots in the streets, the collapse of the world economy, the decline of political morality, the menace of bubonic

11

plague, the erosion of the ozone layer ... Armageddon coming" mark the world in which we live.

A distinguished professor at the Massachusetts Institute of Technology joined four other M.I.T.-Harvard experts in predicting that mankind can expect a nuclear war in the next twenty-five years and that the only way to prohibit this inevitable event is through some "nasty kind of world government." Big choice.

The President of France, Valery Giscard d'Estaing, says, "The world is unhappy. It is unhappy because it doesn't know where it is going and because it senses that, if it knew, it would discover that it was heading for disaster." The list of those who declared doom for mankind includes Malcolm Muggeridge, H. G. Wells, Abba Eban, Henry Kissinger, Albert Schweitzer, Aleksandr Solzhenitsyn, and the Club of Rome.

The Club of Rome, one of the most distinguished collections of intellectuals observing and analyzing the human scene, has concluded that mankind is faced with a number of problems, *every one* of which is capable of destroying the human race in this century. It concludes that mankind, besides being incapable of solving the problems, is totally without the ability even to understand them!

Four point two billion people walk the earth today and probably not even five percent of them are in any position to make an impact on the future destiny of the human race. In the face of this it is no marvel to me that "revolution" is on the lips of millions.[1] They have no solution, but they find it incomprehensible that anything that would replace the present situation could be worse! A pop song of the fifties announced sarcastically that "They're rioting in Africa, they're starving in Spain. . . ." That was the fifties and

---

[1] A good source book for further information on this subject is WWIII: *Signs of the Impending Battle of Armageddon,* by John Wesley White of the Billy Graham Evangelistic Team.

no improvement in either the rioting world or the starving world is visible. In fact, the grim reality of drought, food shortage, population increase and starvation is so bleak as to be nearly unmentionable.

The world is *solutionless.*

Ironic, isn't it, that the world that was offered the King of Kings in the first century and opted to murder him finds its solutions have compounded the problems. Ironic, isn't it, that the one who proved he had the secret to the food problem was framed by the orthodox of his day because he rose above the phony moral standards they professed. He could have fed the whole world with those five loaves and two fishes!

Washington is solutionless. The United Nations is solutionless. The World Bank is solutionless. The world church is solutionless. The world military is solutionless. The world governments are solutionless. The world's intellectuals are solutionless. And where, may I ask, is the Church, the true body of Jesus Christ, in the midst of this? Oh, the church is there arguing over charismatic renewal, the timing and spacing of prophetic events, whether Billy Graham compromises too much, whether parachurch organizations are friends or enemies, and whether divorce is okay when your spouse commits adultery and *you* are the innocent party. As Dr. Bill Bright of Campus Crusade for Christ puts it, we are adjusting pictures on the walls of a burning building.

Imagine. Doing this while we hold in sacred trust *the solution*. Yes, I'll say it again, *the solution*.

The Old Testament prophets knew where the solution would be. It would be in the person of the Messiah. I was riding a bus in New England a few years ago and sat next to a Jewish gentlemen. I asked him if he was looking for the coming of the Jewish Messiah. "Oh yes," he replied. "How will you recognize him when he comes?" I asked. He didn't know, but he was looking. At least he had read the Old Testment and knew that the Messiah would be the solution.

It was a dramatic scene when Jesus went back to his hometown and visited the local synagogue. It appears he rather "took charge" by asking for the scroll that contained the writings of the prophet Isaiah. It was handed to him and he read through it until he came to the spot that contained the solution. He read:

> The Spirit of the Lord is upon me; he has appointed me to preach Good News to the poor; he has sent me to heal the broken-hearted and to announce that captives shall be released and the blind shall see, that the down-trodden shall be freed from their oppressors, and that God is ready to give blessings to all who come to him.

When Jesus had finished reading, he rolled up the scroll, gave it back, and sat down.

I imagine you could have heard a pin drop. He'd only read a few verses from Isaiah 61, a messianic passage which was undoubtedly familiar to the synagogue faithful. You could hear breathing as the assembly listened to what this "home town boy" would say that might confirm or deny the incredible reports they had heard of his miracles in other parts of their land.

He simply stated, "with your very own eyes you have seen these prophetic words come true." He announced the solution. He was the solution! The solution he describes here E. Stanley Jones calls the "kingdom manifesto." It was the total solution to the total world problem.

First, it involved the coming of the Spirit of God upon man. Many Old Testament passages indicate that a mark of the Messiah would be that the Spirit of the Lord would be upon him. The significance of this concern escaped me for nearly twenty years of my Christian life. I had no concept of what it would mean to my life to have the Spirit of the Lord upon (filling, empowering, controlling) me. Oh, don't get me wrong. I hadn't gotten through my Christian home, Bible-teaching church, Christian community, Christian college and seminary without finding out about the Holy Spirit. I remember memorizing pages of Bible references in seminary on the doctrine of the Holy Spirit. But I also remember that when I was asked at my examination for ordination what the difference was between the indwelling of the Holy Spirit and the filling of the Holy Spirit, I didn't know the answer—either intellectually or experientially.

During those years it didn't even impress me that Jesus was able to do supernatural things like love enemies, turn the other cheek, and go the second mile. After all, I reasoned, he was God. It doesn't impress me that God can perform like God. I am a man.

But it was at that point that I was blind. The very point of the kingdom solution is that a mortal, a man, can have the Spirit of God upon him. The immortal, invisible Spirit of the Almighty can pulse through my veins, can excite every corpuscle, guide every thought, superintend every decision, motivate to right responses, and create God's character. Jesus was also a man, and when a man can live like God, that opens up a whole new world of solutions!

In Jesus the ultimate solution was set forth for a supernatural quality of life that would liberate every recipient of his Spirit from the weasely human nature which remains his worst enemy. He was saying, "Today you are seeing that a man can live like God, and I am the example you were told to look for by the Old Testament prophets. Here before you is a mortal in which the Spirit of Jehovah dwells."

They didn't like the implications. They "marvelled at his words," but they were not about to accept his solution.

They had solutions of their own. His solution was spiritual.

Second, the solution Jesus offered was an economic one. He came to preach Good News to the poor.

Jesus was not insensitive to the economic inequities of life. He had not been calloused by the exploitation of the poor by the rich. He didn't like it any more than you or I do that some people squander millions on their grown-up toys (yachts, airplanes, diamonds, etc.) while the poor beg for bread. He understands the Marxists cries against the capitalists who siphon off the cream of societal wealth while the workers suffer. The Marxists did not invent economic compassion.

Indeed, I resent the charge that Christianity has done nothing for the poor but exploit them. I am acutely aware that the seedbed for Communism is corrupt capitalism and corrupt Christianity. But Marxists do not know that what they are seeing is the church, not the Church. The true believers in Jesus have been the vanguard of social action. I'll match the global efforts of Christians to meet the needs of the poor against that of any single group put up for comparison.

But the Marxists have discovered that even if you change the economic structure of society, you do not stop the exploitation of one man by another. That is because the economic solution does not work unless the *spiritual* solution is applied first. No man responds differently to another man because the economy is different, but he does if his spirit is different, if he is controlled by the Spirit of God.

There never has been better news for the poor. Not only is there hope of inheritance of the universe as joint heirs with Christ, there is also the promise of God's economic custody of them while they are here on earth. Jesus promised believers that for those who seek the kingdom as their first priority there is no justification for anxiety about

what they should eat, what they should drink, or what
they should put on (Matthew 6). Those things are "givens."
The Psalmist declared:

> Once I was young but now I am old;
> Yet I have not seen the righteous forsaken
> or his children begging bread (Psalm 37:25).

The scriptures are full of references describing how
God promises to prosper the righteous—economically as
well as spiritually. Jesus made the very thought that the
heavenly Father would forsake the physical needs of his
children as ridiculous as

> an earthly father giving his son a stone when he
>   asked for bread;
> giving a son a snake when he has asked for fish;
> giving a son a scorpion when he has asked for an
>   egg;
> feeding sparrows and letting his own children
>   starve;
> clothing the lilies of the field beautifully and let-
>   ting his own children go naked.

Whenever the spiritual solution is applied, the economic one follows. At Pentecost, a classic case of what happens when thousands of people are simultaneously filled
with the Spirit, Christians "held all possessions in common." The closest thing I have ever witnessed to this was
when the Holy Spirit came upon a group of about fifty in
the jungles of South America. The filling of the Spirit was
so great that one man casually admired his Christian brother's brand new camera only to have to fight off his brother's attempt to give it to him! A lady noticed the beautiful
hand beaded necklace of another lady whereupon the lady
took it off and placed it on the neck of her friend.
The Good News of the kingdom is Good News to the

poor. I don't expect to be rich in worldly goods by Western standards, but I do expect to prosper, to have my needs supplied, to have food, shelter and clothing, and to be rich in spirit. I already am among the wealthiest men in human history.

Third, the solution of the King is a political one. He came to release captives. *"Christian captives of the world, shout; your release has come!"* Jesus was sensitive to the fact that the political systems of the kingdom of darkness would oppress his children, the citizens of his kingdom. They imprisoned him, why would they not imprison his children?

There is no question that more believers in Jesus Christ are being imprisoned, tortured and murdered for their faith in this quarter of a century than in all of the previous history of the Church. Thousands of dead Christians were stacked by the roadside in Cambodia. I read first-person accounts of this massacre from one who escaped. There are hundreds of thousands of Christians being imprisoned under Idi Amin in Uganda, Machel in Mozambique, in Soviet Russia and her satellite countries, Red China, Viet Nam, Cuba, Chile, some Moslem countries and other parts of the world.

The King is not deaf to their cries. He hears the screams from Siberia, the weeping in Africa and the groans from Southeast Asia. He has the Good News of release to captives. "Captives" connotes those citizens of one state that are in exile under the political domination of another. Beautiful. The citizens of the kingdom that are under the domination of an alien political system headed ultimately by the Prince of Darkness will be released. They already are free.

I sat in the office of a Christian brother behind the "Iron Curtain" and listened with awe to his story of ongoing evangelism and discipleship despite constant harassment and even imprisonment from his government. I asked, "What happens if you go to prison?"

He responded deliberately. "I have been in prison for fourteen years under both the Nazis and the Communists. When I was in prison I was a very free man." When he met the King, he discovered the kingdom and its spiritual solution, its economic solution and its political solution. He was *released* and no prison could ever again contain him. Jesus the Liberator had set him free.

Fourth, the kingdom solution is a physical solution. "Recovery of sight to the blind" was an integral part of the Good News. I don't know what it would be like to be blind, but I am looking forward to throwing away my corrective lenses. What a glorious heap that will be—crutches, wheel chairs, eyeglasses, medicine cabinets, trusses, orthopedic shoes, false teeth, iron lungs, kidney machines, pacemakers, hearing aids, artificial limbs, toupees (!), braille writings, walkers, slings, and braces. No need for those in the kingdom.

But again, this remedy is not just for the future. Jesus offers healing to us today. Don't get frightened, I am not about to offer you a healing miracle in exchange for purchasing a prayer hanky or by placing your hands on this book cover! But James 5 makes it clear that there is a scriptural formula for healing—through appropriation of the anointing with oil and the prayer of faith. Prayers of faith have cured more diseases throughout the history of the Church than all of the world's physicians have. The quip is true which says, "God heals; the doctor collects the fee."

I know I am a recipient of his divine physical healing. My release through new birth and the filling of the Spirit has introduced preventive medicine against sixty percent of the maladies which have people ill today. That figure may be conservative. I am talking about those maladies caused directly or indirectly by inner stress, guilt, anxiety, bitterness, fear and other illnesses that have spiritual-psychological origins.

I believe God has healed me on occasions from the

little maladies that have struck. I believe that the "prayer of faith" holds a key to much more physical healing than most of us Christians realize. We just don't pray and we just don't trust. We have the promise that even if he chooses not to heal *now*, his grace is sufficient.

So leap, ye lame! Shout, ye dumb! Listen, ye deaf! Dance, ye paralyzed! You are HEALED! Jesus' solution is *physical* as well as spiritual, economic and political.

Fifth, Jesus offers a solution that is psychological. Can you imagine the collective psychological hurt that the world is suffering at any given moment? Can you fathom the compounded inner destruction of living in a system that is dominated by evil and by the principles of the anti-kingdom? God can. He can *never* escape the aggregate emotional suffering and psychological destruction that has taken creatures made "in his image" and perverted them beyond recognition. We can avoid, repress, forget, deny or escape, but an all-knowing and omnipresent God can never brush aside the grim reality of all this mental anguish.

"To set at liberty them that are bruised" fails to communicate what must have been the mind of the Spirit when this was penned. The Aramaic version says "To strengthen with forgiveness them that are bruised." The bruising referred to here is psychological and can only be cured by the extension of God's forgiveness to every aspect of a person's personality. R. C. H. Lenski in his commentary on this biblical narrative translates this "to send the broken away in a state of (total) release." He explains, "Sin wrecks and makes wretched by its crushing, shattering consequences in this life and the Savior ... frees from wretchedness and restores joy and peace."

Now tell me, have you ever heard of a solution that was this total? Not even the tiniest vestige of psychological hurt is left when Christ's solution is applied! All of the fears, anxieties, sorrows and persecution, all the self-images marred through ridicule and harassment are taken care of by the King.

This also is in the present tense. The kingdom solution makes lovers out of murderers, companions out of enemies, and whole people out of fragments. It removes guilt, assures us of God's unconditional love and acceptance, gives the recognition we all long for, and sustains an unbroken and intimate relationship which can never be severed. It floods a broken psyche with love and the "renewing of the mind." What a solution!

So there we have it: the irony of a solutionless world and the kingdom solution, existing side by side in the same situation. I'd like to shout it at the United Nations, blanket the TV screens of the world with it, write it on the walls of Red Square, plaster it in posters on the buildings of Peking. But if I did, how would the nations of the world respond? They'd reject the solution. They rejected the King; they'll continue to reject his kingdom. Remember, they have their *own* "solutions."

Proverbs 26:11 tells us why. "As a dog returns to its vomit, so a fool returns to his folly." Return, O World, but know that there *is* a better way.

I saw the essence of this solution written on the walls of a city. In Latin America amid the revolutionary grafitti I saw written, "Solo Jesus Hace Un Hombre Nuevo." Only Jesus makes a man new. This *is* the solution.

3 A Kingdom Mentality Shapes the World

Every society has some variety of social pyramid. This pyramid results from the "stacking" of the people within the society by social class with social class determined by the possession of wealth, power, and knowledge. The masses of poor are at the bottom as the "base" of the pyramid. The middle classes are in the central portion of the pyramid and are usually smaller in number than the lower classes which comprise the base. At the top of the pyramid is a tiny apex varying from one or two percent to ten percent. These are the people who possess most of the wealth, power and knowledge. This group runs the society.

A friend of mine, a powerful person, says, "if you work at the top of the pyramid, you don't have to move so far to get things done." And, in so saying, he describes the reality of both the present and the past. The people at the top of the pyramid have been the ones that have shaped history. They may not have started out in life at the top of the pyramid, but they got to the top before they really began to change the course of history.

But even among the "top five percenters" there have been world changers in special ways. Many have been kings, but not many kings have significantly changed the course of history. Many have been governors, but few have made an impact on the course of human events and the lives of those outside their realms. Those few who have been world changers have possessed an attribute that was more significant than being born into or penetrating the ranks of the top five percent. They possessed a "kingdom mentality."

Those individuals who possess a kingdom mentality can be described as having the following attributes:

1. A conquering world view;
2. A commitment to a cause with global dimensions;
3. A conviction of invincibility;
4. A sense of divine sanction for what they were doing;
5. An unwillingness to accept the status quo as unalterable;
6. A vision or dream of what the world could be like and a determination to make the dream reality.

Some of history's "world changers" have possessed nearly all of the above dimensions. Some just a few. But I venture to say that none has made a significant impact on the world without any of the above attributes.

The man who, legend says, sat down and wept because there were no more worlds to conquer was Alexander the Great. Alexander the Third, King of Macedonia from 336 to 323 B.C., is credited with introducing a whole new age of human history, the Hellenistic age. Alexander was born into the top five percent. He was the son of King Philip II of Macedonia and stepped into his place in history when his father was assassinated. Alexander systematically did away with his foes and established an empire that extended eastward as far as India, northward as far as Scythia, and southward as far as Egypt and the Persian gulf. He never lost a single battle!

What drove the man to conquer? He had a kingdom mentality. Historical accounts describe Alexander as being "seized by a longing" to explore and reach the unknown, whether of the earth or of the spirit. The Greek historian,

Polybius, described him as a man "by universal consent of a superhuman elevation of spirit."

Alexander spoke of himself as having a mission to reconcile the world and he prayed that Persians and Macedonians would always live as equal partners. Plutarch said that Alexander "believed that he came as a heaven-sent harmonizer and reconciler for the whole world."

The impact of Alexander's conquests prepared the way for the coming of the true King. Because of Alexander the New Testament was written in Greek. One of the earliest centers for biblical research and scholarship was "Alexandria" and one of its products the Greek Old Testament, the Septuagint.

Alexander possessed an unshakable commitment that an improved world order could result and that he could be used to establish that new order. He believed that there were spiritual forces that had placed him in a position to conquer. And he did, though he lived only to age thirty-three.

Genghis Khan was one of the world's great conquerors. He was a ruler of the Mongols and led his armies from China to Russia. He penetrated westward into Iran and Afghanistan. But the picture we see from history of the Mongol barbarians obscures that driving motivation of Genghis.

His name started him on this pursuit of a conquering world view. He was named Temujin after a Tatar chief that his father killed shortly before Genghis' birth. This was done because of the belief that the valor of a defeated enemy magically entered the newborn. He lived up to the name given him and was a warrior at age fifteen when he married and spent twenty years rising to become khan, or "chief" of the Mongols. In another twenty years he had come to dominate the political and military scene of that era.

But his was not just the ruthless and rapacious course of a bloodthirsty military man. He sensed that there were solutions in the realm of the spirit. The title of Genghis Khan, which could variously be translated "chief of the oceans," or perhaps even "world chief", gave him the reason to pursue those spiritual answers.

He sought the secret to immortality from a Taoist priest and asked for an explanation of the Muslim religion by the learned divines of Bukhara. He pursued the philosophy that a nomadic warrior elite should remain in the steppes exacting tribute from the conquered kingdoms of the world. At one point in history he inquired through Marco Polo if the Pope would send one hundred teachers that were well learned in the seven arts and "able to prove that the way of Christ was best." The Pope foolishly proposed, through the *two* teachers that he sent, that Genghis Khan become attached to Rome as both a political and a religious subject.

Genghis obviously rejected the proposal and adopted Islam, which he spread throughout the worlds he conquered. No man could kill his kingdom mentality and the Pope failed to channel it to the eternal kingdom of our Lord Jesus Christ. A nomadic Mongolian warrior shook the world because he had a kingdom mentality.

Another of history's powerhouses was a little man, a scrawny, yellow-faced, badly-dressed man. By age twenty-six hardly anyone had heard his name. Yet this man is legendary as a conqueror. He rose to such popularity that his nation's people gave him virtually unlimited power. He instituted codes of government and law that exist today, a century and a half after his death. His memory is glorified in the annals of political and military history. His name is Napoleon.

I don't have to recount for you the exploits of this man in Italy (where he was appointed commander in chief of military forces), Egypt, Syria, Russia, Austria, Belgium, Holland and Germany (where General Mack was forced to surrender to him). The armies of France under Napoleon seemed for some time invincible. Waterloo proved the contrary. But this man left his indelible print on the history of Europe and the world.

What drove Napoleon? At the age of twenty-two, while studying at Valence, he wrote an essay on the topic "What are the principles and institutions most likely to bring about the greatest happiness of mankind?" It was this man that took command of the Italian army, thirty thousand starving soldiers in need of everything. To them he said, "You are badly fed and all but naked. . . . I am about to lead you into the most fertile plains in the world. . . . There we shall find honor, glory and riches." A crazy man? No, he just possessed a kingdom mentality.

Dying in exile on Saint Helena he was still a conqueror. "We are martyrs to an immortal cause," he said. "We struggle against oppression and the voice of the nations is for us." While a political prisoner he made himself the apostle of a political doctrine based on the principles of liberty, equality, fraternity and justice. He identified his cause with that of universal freedom. "Though they are scattered, there are thirty million Frenchmen, fifteen million Italians, and thirty million Germans. I should like to have made of each of these a single nation."

Napoleon was gone but his remains were later returned to France to be enshrined in the Invalides. In large part due to the legend which Napoleon wrote, his nephew was elected president after the revolution of 1848 and then restored the empire. You can't even destroy a kingdom mentality by death and burial.

I could go on to describe Spain's "invincible Armada." I could tell of the vision of a British Empire upon which "the sun would never set." But a few more examples will suffice.

The first is from my earliest recollections. I can still remember the terror which filled my heart as we in mid-Ohio cut the lights, pulled the blinds, and peered anxiously out the windows as the town alarm system had warned us to do. These were called "air raid drills" and were civil defense protection.

Protection against whom? Against a German politician named Adolf Hitler. He seemed a most unlikely sort of person to be frightening the socks off a five-year-old boy in Lexington, Ohio, all the way across an ocean. But we didn't know if Hitler's Luftwaffe might attack our shores as it had the territory of so many other nations.

I can still hear the recordings on the radio of Hitler addressing the masses (sometimes numbering more than half a million) in Berlin. I can hear the ringing of "Heil Hitler" in my ears and can see the goosestepping troops marching in the movie newsreels.

But how could a mustachioed, erratic, former paper hanger have brought millions under his sway? How could he have built a political and military machine that could set about internally to eradicate nearly six million arbitrarily-determined enemies? How could he have done this without the populace vomiting him out of office?

There can be only one answer. He had a kingdom mentality. He had inflamed the minds of his people with his dream of a new era, a one-thousand-year rule and reign of the Aryan peoples. I remember seeing an architect's conceptions of the glories of the Third Reich. One such picture was of a great domed stadium that would seat one *million* people. It made the great domed arenas of this day look like anterooms. When any leader can inflame the minds of his people with a kingdom mentality, they will pay any sacrifice, set aside personal objectives, and over-look weaknesses (even blindly) in pursuit of the *cause*.

How do you think a handful of Marxists have suc-ceeded in threatening the entire globe? How have they been able to capture one half of the world's territory and one third of its people? How? Easy. They have a kingdom mentality. They know that it is "inevitable" that the cap-italist systems will collapse. These systems are under a *historical imperative* to succumb to socialist systems until the entire globe will be under the rule of the dictatorship of the proletariat—the worker. The common man will rule the world!

Guerrillas in the hills of South America are inflamed by that thought. College students disillusioned by the cor-ruption of Watergates are stirred by the concept. Every person who has ever been exploited by the rich or resented the inequitable distribution of wealth and power in his country is moved to embrace the idealism of world rule by the worker.

Mao, the patron saint of Communism, ruling the most populous nation in the world, made it clear that it was a kingdom mentality that motivated him to conquer. He stated in the Bible of Red China, *Quotations from Chairman Mao*:

> What kind of spirit is this that makes a foreigner self-lessly adopt the cause of the Chinese people's liberation as his own? It is the spirit of internationalism, the spirit of communism, from which every Chinese Communist must learn. . . . We must unite with the proletariat of all countries. . . to liberate the other nations and peoples of the world.

E. Stanley Jones relays the story of his visit to Moscow. He watched as workers carried dirt up out of the ground for the building of a subway. They were chanting as they worked, and Jones inquired the meaning of their chant. He was told they were chanting, "We are building a new world." A kingdom mentality. At the level of a ditchdigger, a concept that every deed and action was building a new world!

I think you can trace the vitality of religious as well as political movements to a kingdom mentality. It's no mystery to me why I have my door pounded twice a year or more by Jehovah's Witnesses. They are committed to the concept of the kingdom. They don't attend churches, remember. They attend *Kingdom Halls.* They are part (through some specious reasoning which I could never jibe with Scripture) of the 144,000 divinely-appointed witnesses on the earth to prepare the way for the kingdom. If the Church just once again got infected with that kingdom disease we would outpound the Jehovah's Witnesses any day!

Did you catch that? I said once *again.* It did happen once, you know. The first century Church was infected with a chronic case of kingdom disease—it possessed a kingdom mentality.

There was electricity in the air when Peter rose to speak on the day of Pentecost. Supernatural events had marked the day. The sound like a mighty rushing wind. The tongues of fire. The communication to each present in his own language whether or not it had been spoken. The onlookers were baffled and resorted to scoffing at the proceedings as Peter took the floor. Get this. This is the same Peter that a few days earlier was so frightened to admit that he was a follower of Christ that he shrank from an inquiring maiden and cursed, denying his master three times in a single twenty-four-hour period!

"Fellow Jews and all of you who are in Jerusalem. . . ," he began. Then he proceeded to lay out for them a bold defense of the kingship of Christ punctuated by three Old Testament prophecies. In the first quote he pointed out what would happen before "the coming of the great and glorious day of the Lord." This is a second coming and kingdom reference.

Then he reminded them from the words of David that death could not hold sway over the King. He concluded with a real blockbuster of a passage for a bunch that had just murdered the Messiah. He pointed out that this risen King had assumed a position at the right hand of the Father (they knew that was *the* position in the royal throneroom) and that the King would not rest until he had made his enemies his footstools or, in modern parlance, "made mincemeat" of his enemies.

The logical question they asked was, "Brothers, what shall we do?" Peter said, "Repent." They did, three thousand of them before sundown!

You see, they were shook. They should have been. They murdered the King of Kings. So they decided they had better join him before he beat them. And join him they did. They went preaching the good news of the risen King all over the world. They created such a stir in their hometown that it wasn't long before they were clamped in chains, whereupon they delivered a little talk on the King and the absolute authority he possessed. "Salavation," they said, "is found in no one else." And the ecclesiastical leaders that had arrested them "were astonished" when they saw their "boldness." Up until that time, you see, the priests had never observed a Christian with a kingdom mentality.

After the release of Peter and John, there was a great prayer and praise rally at which they prayed,

> Sovereign Lord, you made the heaven and the earth and the sea, and everything in them. You spoke by the Holy Spirit through the mouth of your servant, our father David, "What good does it do if the nations rant and rave and the people engage in useless plots against you? The Kings of the earth dig in their heels and the

rulers conspire against the Lord of Lords and the King
of Kings, and against his Christ! How ridiculous!"
(Acts 4:24-26 author's paraphrase)

The illustrations I have given here could be multiplied
inside and outside the Church a thousand times. Nothing
happens to a man to bring him to change the world until he
begins to challenge the way things are, dream of what
could be, and put his life on the line to make it happen. In
the words of George Bernard Shaw, "Some men look at
what is and say, 'Why?' I look at what could be and say,
'Why not?' "

A conquering world view, commitment to a global
cause, conviction of invincibility, divine sanction, and a
vision of what the world could be like make up a kingdom
mentality. Christians have more reason for it and less of it
than any group on earth. Businessmen pursue everything
from the building of motels to the marketing of hamburg-
ers with a kingdom mentality. They succeed because they
set out with the belief that it can and should be done to the
place where it borders on the ridiculous.

At a meeting in Europe of Christians from more than a
dozen European countries the German master of ceremo-
nies asked with a twinkle in his eyes, "What are the three
universal Christian words, words that are the same in any
language?" He waited a moment for thought and then
offered, "Hallelujah is number one, Amen is number two,
and the last is . . . COCA-COLA!" I have an acquaintance
who is an executive in the Coca-Cola Company. They just
celebrated their fiftieth anniversary as the most widely
marketed and widely accepted product in the history of the
world. The aging founder lived to see his dream. He had a
kingdom mentality of sorts.

I sat in the office of a businessman in South Florida, a
successful businessman. On his wall he had a plaque with a
statement which was headed by the words, "I do not
choose to be a common man." The statement described his

desire to rise above the masses, achieve greater excellence, and leave bolder imprints on the "sands of time." I thought, no one ever challenged me to be more than a common Christian, to pursue in practical ways a kingdom of mentality. So I drafted my own statement:

I DO NOT CHOOSE TO BE A "COMMON" CHRISTIAN

I cannot separate my faith in Jesus of Nazareth from my everyday life, conduct, and speech.

I cannot justify loving only those who love me, aiding only my friends, and praying only for fellow Christians.

I have no desire to carry the name of the Son of God to the level of my own base intentions.

I aspire to be like Him, to live on unseen resources by faith, to tap the unlimited supply of His love through the life of His indwelling Holy Spirit, to emerge from my moral conflicts "more than a conqueror" through His power, and to rise above all earthly standards to the completeness of His perfection.

I acknowledge that this is an impossible quest but accept the challenge of its impossibility in the knowledge that its pursuit will force me to rest on Him.

I desire no little challenges, expect no unrippled seas, and abandon all personal "rights."

I consider it a curse to have a quality of life that is indistinguishable from unbelieving men and common Christians.

My present failure to fulfill these intentions merely proves that God isn't finished reshaping my raw materials.

This thinking has changed my life. It can change yours. Not because it is my thinking, but because it is the *King's* thinking. A kingdom mentality is the King's mentality.

4 The Grounding of the Gospel

The world had not seen such unrestrained zeal, such total commitment, such boldness in the proclamation of a message. It all came out of Pentecost, this overwhelming spiritual power which the followers of Jesus exhibited. Jesus had told them that it would be this way. He told them that they would receive power after the Holy Spirit had come upon them, and power they possessed! Sick people were healed, thousands were ushered into the kingdom of Jesus Christ, even dead people were raised to life.

Jesus was so emphatic about their need for power in the beginning that he required them to stay home until they had received the promise of the Father and were "clothed with power from on high" (Luke 24:49). They stayed home and waited, and they were glad they had. The new era of the Holy Spirit's work in their lives provided a supernatural impact to their message that nothing could minimize or restrain. The dark sayings from the lips of Jesus became living truths. The mysterious parables became clear concepts revolutionizing lives, changing families, bringing together communities of believers, and shaking the pagan foundations of the culture in which they lived.

Just to make sure that they did not miss the importance of the teachings on the kingdom, Jesus spent forty days with them *after* his resurrection and *before* Pentecost "speaking to them things concerning the kingdom of God." That must have been some forty-day Bible conference! The risen Messiah explained some of the things that he had told them before but that they could not understand without the perspective which the resurrection provided.

33

They learned their lessons well. In Acts 8 Phillip is in Samaria (of all places) amazing the people with the mighty works which God is doing through him. Through his ministry many believe and are baptized as he preaches "the good news of the kingdom of God and the name of Jesus Christ." In Acts 14 Paul and Barnabas are in Antioch in Syria encouraging the disciples there with the declaration that "we must go through many hardships to enter the kingdom of God."

In Acts 19 Paul is at Ephesus. There he finds it appropriate to spend *three months* in the synagogue "speaking boldly" and "arguing persuasively about the kingdom of God." When the reaction to his message was mixed, Paul changed quarters and held daily discussions in the lecture hall of Tyrannus. This he did for *two more years!* At the end of his time in Ephesus, Paul gave a very tearful, but very forceful, parting address. He assured the believers that he was confident and that he was innocent of the blood of all men. He had been forgiven because he had been faithful to "preach the kingdom" and, in so doing to "proclaim the whole will of God (Acts 20:25-27)."

The Apostle Paul did the same things with the Roman Christians. In a dramatic final move near the end of his life he called the Jewish leaders together even while he was under heavy Roman guard. He explained how he got to Rome in chains, and "from morning till evening explained and declared to them the kingdom of God and tried to convince them about Jesus from the Law of Moses and from the Prophets (Acts 28:23 NIV)."

Fitting the good news of salvation into the context of the building of the kingdom of God gave the gospel its "oomph." The whole message of the gospel is not just that a man can have eternal fire insurance. It is to let him know that he can be born into a kingdom that is under the rule and reign of the world's first perfectly righteous ruler. This takes the gospel out of the realm of "pie in the sky by and by" and makes it relevant to every human being in a practical and immediate way. From new birth on every step he takes and every thought he thinks can be contributing to the building of this new world order and preparing for the return of his King who will put it all together.

Jesus never omitted the dimension of the kingdom from the preaching of the Good News. Jesus, in one way or another, referred to the kingdom more than 100 times in the Gospels! From the beginning to the end of his ministry he was preaching the good news of the kingdom. When his accusers wanted to pin a charge on him that they knew they had evidence to support, they told the Roman authorities, "He calls himself a king." He died with the statement above his head, "The King of the Jews," which statement Pilate refused to alter to "He says he's the King of the Jews." Pilate knew something from his encounter with Jesus that multitudes in the professing Christian world have yet to learn or to incorporate in their "good news."

Jesus began his public ministry by declaring "Repent, the kingdom of heaven is at hand" (Matthew 4:17). He began "preaching the gospel of the kingdom" and launched his sermonic ministry with a presentation of the spiritual character of kingdom life. We call this presentation the Sermon on the Mount. He taught his followers to pray that the kingdom of God would be established on earth just as it is in heaven (Matthew 6:10). He told his disciples to declare that "the kingdom of heaven is at hand" (Matthew 10:7), and related a score of parables explaining various dimensions of the kingdom.

One such collection of parables is contained in Matthew 13. Even after years of extensive seminary training I still viewed Matthew 13 as a confusing mess of obscure and oblique parables. But in 1975 the Spirit of God illumined my mind in a single evening and this chapter became a turning point in my life and ministry. While some of the keys of that passage will be explained later, one gem is critical at this point.

Jesus explained the parable he had told about the seed that fell on varying kinds of ground. You remember the parable. The seed that fell on good ground multiplied and the seed that fell on poor ground didn't. In explaining the parable to his disciples, he remarked that the receptivity of the soil is analogous to understanding "the message about the kingdom." Consequently, the person who hears "the message about the kingdom" and *doesn't understand it* is like the hardened ground near the path which is unproductive. The person who receives the word of the kingdom with excitement but doesn't let it penetrate to a deeper level is like the soil that is rocky, shallow and not conducive to deep roots. The person that receives the word of the kingdom but gets distracted by the cares and attractions of the world system (wealth, etc.), is like thorny soil. It is the man that *"hears* the word (of the kingdom) *and understands it"* that becomes productive thirty, sixty, or one hundred times over.

The moral of this story seems to be that a person's whole vitality as a Christian—his depth and his ultimate productivity in the lives of others—is correlated with the extent to which he has *heard* and *understood* the good news of *the kingdom!*

This helps me understand a lot of phenomena of my Christian experience that I didn't understand before. It explains to me why some Christians are so on fire, sold out, one hundred percent, and hanging in there for the long run. They *heard* and *understood* the good news of the kingdom. They are not involved in some vague religious system. They are not part of a social club with ethical overtones. They are not identified with some warmed-over version of the YMCA. They are fully aware that they are involved in a vital relationship with a *King* who is *right now through them* building his kingdom.

This also helps me understand why in our country evangelical schools, seminaries and churches are growing "like mad" while the involvement curve on the liberal, non-kingdom institutions is falling off. Even secular sources are amazed at the growth and dynamism of segments of the evangelical movement in North America. They are also non-plussed at the wet Kleenex brand of Christianity proffered in circles where the King isn't even God and his kingdom is some kind of targetless social action or political reform.

One secular source analyzing the various kinds of Christian educational institutions commented that:

> Too often, in Protestant colleges, the content of chapel services is a vague humanitarianism which does justice neither to the majesty of God nor the intellectual aspirations of a college.

This "vague humanitarianism" has turned more seriously inquiring Christians away from Christ than could ever be counted. No Christian wants to be involved simply in a lukewarm system of fuzzy humanistic programs for the betterment of mankind. A person who is attracted to the the person and message of Jesus of Nazareth wants to be involved in a system that enthrones him as King and shares his supernatural power with all those who grant entrance to his life-giving Spirit.

Madeline Murray O'Hair went to a Christian college which, at the time, was wallowing in "a vague humanitarianism." Madeline has a "kingdom mentality." She is out to change her world! I can't help thinking she would be on the other side of the atheism controversy if she had ever *heard* and *understood* the Good News of the kingdom of Jesus Christ!

But that is the story of the success and failure of the Gospel. When the Good News of the kingdom is presented in the full context of God's eternal plan, including his plan for establishing his rule on earth through his Messiah King, then the Gospel has *impact*. You remove the concept of the kingdom from the good news of salvation and you provide for new believers a limp-wristed, mushy and amorphous system into which they channel the glories of new birth, Holy Spirit baptism, and identification with the Church.

You can trace the loss of the concept of the kingdom to many tragedies in the history of the Church. E. Stanley Jones makes this point powerfully:

> Call the roll of the tragedies in history and they all root in that loss of the kingdom. Take Israel, when it was said of her; "the kingdom of God will be taken away from you and given to a nation producing the fruits of it" (Matthew 21:43 RSV). That refusal on the part of Israel became the long tragedy of a frustrated nation. Take the Crusades—men of violence tried to take that kingdom by force and succeeded in laying the foundation of hate and conflicts through the centuries. Take Genghis Khan's request through Marco Polo to the Pope: "Please send us a hundred teachers, well learned in the seven arts and well able to prove that the way of Christ is best." Marco Polo, seeing the request was of great significance, hastened back to the Pope. Two years later, two teachers instead of 100 were sent with this message, "Become politically and ecclesiastically attached to Rome." They didn't offer the kingdom of God, a universal kingdom; they offered a political and ecclesiastical attachment to Rome. Genghis Khan turned it down, accepted Islam, and spread blood and fire and a hating faith through Asia and Europe.
>
> When Russia was in the throes of a revolution, instead of the church offering the kingdom of God on earth, a church council was debating the question of

whether garments of a certain color should be used in a certain place in the church service and debating *that* while Russia was turning red! In Italy the nation was not offered a universal kingdom, the kingdom of God, but a papal, ecclesiastical system instead, so Italy made the state supreme, chose fascism, and brought the nation into defeat and collapse. Germany chose Nazism, making the race supreme; when the church offered the kingdom in heaven hereafter, it brought its own ruin.

When, in the welter of conflicts, America arose supreme out of the chaos, we offered "the American way of life," instead of God's way of life, *the kingdom of God*, and are ending up plagued by our own racial, class and economic conflicts, with little to offer the world. The Church is largely to blame because the Church, instead of offering the kingdom of God, offered various conflicts—fundamental-modernist; the social gospel-the individual gospel; racial integration; the secular church; long hair-short hair; beards and non-beards; the church-building orgy; then vestments and candles and robes; conversion; abolition of poverty and ghettos—every issue except the kingdom of God.[1]

Joe Bayly in one of his books gives the parable of Herbert Gooley, a college undergraduate that one day began to exhibit a stunning ability, the ability to *fly*. He caused a stir among the university community as he soared out of third-story windows and buzzed the gatherings on the campus mall. Though reaction to Gooley's new-found ability was mixed, some expressed interest in the art and entreated Gooley to teach them how to practice this supernatural ability. Gooley taught them and soon there were squadrons of collegians soaring over the campus.

The faculty responded to the new interest in flying by

[1] E. Stanley Jones, *The Unshakable Kingdom and the Unchanging Person* (Abingdon, 1972), p.18f.

establishing a lecture series on aviation and aeronautical principles. A learned professor taught the lectures day after day but lost complete credibility when, after a visit to the president's office, he *walked* down from the third floor of the administration building! Nobody was interested in aviation theory when there was the slightest possibility that he might be able to *fly*. There was no impact to the learned professor's words, theories and system of thought so long as there was the remotest possibility that students might be involved in something that could lift them into the realm of the supernatural.

So it is with the church. The world couldn't care less whether we are pre-trib, post-trib, a-trib, on-mill, off-mill, or yea-mill. Understanding and "rightly dividing" the Word of truth *is* important to Bible believers. But when we lose the *kingdom* in the theological gamesmanship, we write *mene, mene, tekel, upharsin* on the wall of our banquet hall as in Belshazzar's. At that point the church is "weighed in the balances and found wanting." The church loses it ability to soar above all mankind with supernatural power, a supernatural plan and a supernatural system. It is, at that point, *grounded*.

I could take you to a part of the Church that is pulsating with vitality because it has not lost the concept of the kingdom. Fifteen thousand people a month are trusting Jesus Christ. They are shaking the strongholds of the Marxists on the university campuses. They are facing plots on the lives of their leadership, even physical abuse and violence, unbowed and unbroken. They are invincible in Jesus and in the power of his life. They are shaking the social foudations of a city of one million that is known for its immorality and it prostitution. The growth of the movement has been so dramatic that Roman Catholics on one side and Protestants on the other are threatened.

I think I know why. This movement of the gospel has an aura of invincibility about it. You see, the top leadership was converted from the leadership of the Communist revolution. The top leader was exiled from his homeland for his political activity. He fled to the country where he now lives and met a person that introduced him to the King of Kings and to a new kind of revolution, a spiritual revolution in the hearts of men.

Now despite public false accusations (the press was accusing the leader of being a drug pusher) and threats on his life, the leader and the movement press on preaching the gospel in the power of the Holy Spirit. They square off against all world systems with the confidence of the kingdom of God. They have a kingdom mentality and they refuse to be grounded.

5 The Gate to Conquest

A kingdom mentality. I have been using the phrase in a variety of contexts so far and only with a general definition drawn from the glimpse we took into the lives of some of the world's great conquerors. But, if the definition of a kingdom mentality can be viewed as general for non-Christians, it is very specific for the Christian. You see, a kingdom mentality takes the Christian out of vague, purposeless, religious, piosity and involves him in specific action points that are both clear and relevant to the world dilemma.

For the Christian the kingdom mentality is pointed and objective. It is:

AN UNSHAKABLE COMMITMENT TO THE SOVEREIGNTY OF JESUS CHRIST AND TO THE GROWING ESTABLISHMENT OF HIS INVINCIBLE AND PERFECT WORLD ORDER.

This definition has a number of facets which must be examined to clearly understand the whole concept.

An Unshakable Commitment

No alien becomes a citizen of the United States of America unless (1) he desires to, (2) he commits himself, and (3) he is approved. In the same way no one becomes a part of the kingdom of Jesus Christ unless he desires to, he commits himself, and he meets the requirements and is approved for entrance. God has not been at all secretive about how a person goes about getting into the kingdom. It is a matter of commitment.

The first issue of this commitment is the issue of repentance. Jesus taught, as did his disciples, "Repent, the kingdom of God is at hand." No one gains entrance to the kingdom until he is ready to "come clean," to deal with the wrong in his life, and to change his mind about a lot of things. I say "change his mind" because that is precisely what the word repentance means.

The world is full of people (and the church has plenty too) who are eager to come to the kingdom if they do not have to do away with some pet beliefs. They would, for example, like to accept the King as *a* way to God, and it is not until they come to accept him as *the* way to God that their commitment is sufficient. There are many shadings of belief, but only one shade is acceptable. That shade is *pure white*. That means that a person must repent of every single notion, attitude, or conviction that runs counter to the exclusive right of Jesus to be King. Many are intellectually "rich young rulers" of their own lives who "go away sorrowing" when told they have to repent (change their minds) about the way to eternal life, sell all their alternative ways of salvation, and give them to the poor.

Saving faith, the kind that is acceptable to the King, is an unshakable and unswerving commitment to repent. I did not say change *behavior* because it is equally clear that entrance to the kingdom is a matter of trust, not works. Obviously this is no problem to the King, because he knows that if you have made an unshakable commitment to repent, your behavior will show it forever after.

A second issue of this commitment is that it is to be childlike. In Matthew 19:13-14 Jesus demanded that little children not be kept away because "of such as these is the kingdom of heaven." There is a guilelessness, a transparency and a simplicity with which a commitment to the King must be made. I have a very clever, even cunning, unbelieving friend who keeps trying to "strike deals" with God. At this point he appears still to be outside the kingdom. He'll stay out until he comes without his cunning—until he comes as a dependent, simple, transparent, little child. No one enters the kingdom with his fingers crossed.

A third issue of this commitment is that of accepting the invitation. Matthew 22 records Jesus' kingdom parable of the invitation by the king to his son's wedding feast. The invited guests refused to come, so he extended more invitations until it was clear they were not going to accept. When they did violence to the messengers, the king sent out soldiers to destroy them. Then he opened the invitation to anyone who would come, and many guests, "both good and bad," responded.

Everything was going all right until one guest was found that did not have on appropriate dress for the wedding. He was thrown out. No one stays at the wedding feast without being clothed in the righteous apparel that the king provides. Thus, no one enters the kingdom without making a definite commitment to accept the invitation *and* the appropriate dress.

When I was the president of a college, I saw a long-haired youth sitting cross-legged on our campus as I walked toward the administration building. I stepped off the sidewalk and under the tree where the youth was sitting and began to talk to him about the things of Christ. I invited him to the president's office and caused a few questions as this long-haired, unscrubbed young man followed me into the attractive, carpeted comfort of my office. I presented the claims of Christ to him and then challenged him to accept Jesus' offer of salvation. Apparently the Holy Spirit had made the issues clear, for just when it appeared that he was about to say "yes" to Jesus, he stopped his word and said, "Wait a minute, if I do this, will I have to give up my sex life?"

He was on the threshold of the kingdom. The invitation of the King had been made clear enough that he knew he had to be prepared to "dress accordingly" if he accepted the invitation. "I don't know what your sex life is like, my friend," I replied, "but you cannot enter unless you are willing to do *anything* Christ asks you to do. If he asks you to change your sex life, you must change it. And I can assure you that whatever he asks you to do, he'll provide the power to do." He accepted the invitation with a willingness to dress any way the King dictated. He entered the kingdom.

When an individual makes a *repentant, childlike acceptance* of the offer of the King to rule his life, then the King responds by performing a miracle to "dress him up" for his feasts. That miracle is new birth. Remember that the issue that motivated Nicodemus to his late night rendezvous with Jesus was who this person really was. Messiah? King? Fraud? He came with the conviction that, at the very least, he was a "teacher come from God." Jesus made the issue clear by declaring, "unless a man is born again, he cannot see the kingdom of God." New birth, God's response to man's acceptance.

Even after a person is born into the kingdom, these basic issues don't change. Many a born-again Christian is not captured by a kingdom mentality because he has sin in his life and alien beliefs for which he will not repent. He may lack a simple, childlike trust. He may not, having accepted the initial invitation, be willing to accept other invitations the King may be giving him to enter more deeply into kingdom affairs. Without an *unshakable commitment*, no one experiences a kingdom mentality.

The Sovereignty of Jesus Christ

I have never been impressed by the arguments of one school of evangelists over the issue they call "Lordship salvation." They make a strong pitch for the premise that we must present Jesus as *Savior* to unbelievers, but not as *Lord*. Their reasoning is that if we insist that a person accept the Lordship of Christ when he first believes, it is tantamount to asking him to change his behavior. This, they argue, is salvation by works, and violates the principle of salvation by faith alone.

I have never been impressed by those arguments. I don't believe you can so neatly slice the roles which Christ performs in two. The beloved person who has been my wife for fifteen years plays many roles. When I made a commitment to her I did not, indeed could not, divide her roles and say, "Now I will accept you as wife and lover, but I will not accept you as homemaker and mother." In the same way, when we come to Jesus of Nazareth, we come to one who is, at the same time, Savior, Lord, King, Friend, Co-heir, Disciplinarian, Lover, and a hundred other things. Just as I felt it important to tell that young man that he had to be prepared to deal with his sex life if Christ dealt with him on that issue, I feel that every unbeliever ought to know what he's getting when he comes to Christ.

Whether we hide it, whisper it, or shout it to one on the threshold of the kingdom, sooner or later he is going to find out that Jesus Christ is *Lord—Lord Of Lords. He is Sovereign*.

I have never seen anyone become a world changer until he has totally and completely acknowledged that this Jesus demands and commands control over every dimension of his existence. I have challenged thousands to establish Jesus Christ as Lord through the following commitment:

> Lord, I'll do anything you want me to do, go anywhere you want me to go, say anything you want me to say, and give away anything you want me to give away.

I have watched this commitment give a shot of life and vitality to dying Christians, clean up moral messes in families and separate a person from his phony attachments to job, locale, children, possessions and status. This commitment has liberated more Christians to a kingdom mentality than any other I have observed.

As someone has said, "If Jesus Christ is not Lord *of* all, he is not Lord *at* all." If Jesus Christ is Lord of all, he squares off with the mighty nations and wins. He squares off with the occult forces in the universe and wins. He squares off with Satan himself and wins. He squares off with your problems and wins. He squares off with your enemies and wins. He squares off with every false intellectual system and ideology and wins.

I can't get all excited about committing my life and destiny to a "gentle Jesus, meek and mild" if that is his only side. That excites me about as much as oatmeal without salt. The world has too many dynamic leaders to follow to line up behind some shrunken-faced, mystical creature who couldn't beat his way out of a Jello salad. My King is a sovereign, a tender, loving, compassionate person who has standards and who pursues the enemies of justice with all the mighty potency of the heavens.

The Roman centurion, whose act of faith is recorded in Matthew 8, saw a sovereign in Christ. He told Christ that he was acquainted with sovereignty and that he knew how a sovereign rules, an order is given and the order is obeyed! On that premise he requested that the sovereign of all physical laws merely "give the order" and the paralysis that was plaguing his servant would go away. He knew that laws of nature did not dare defy the order of the *Sovereign* of nature! That is a kingdom mentality.

But Jesus gave us a caution about this whole lordship issue. He warned us against drawing the conclusion that *professing* Jesus as Lord means that in actuality Jesus *is* Lord. He said, "Not everyone that *says* to me 'Lord, Lord,' will enter the kingdom of heaven, but only he who *does* the will of my Father who is in heaven" (Matthew 7:21). Satan laughs when a person professes Christ as Lord but actually lets everything else rule his life.

Even the thief on the cross saw sovereignty in Christ. He wasn't fooled by the battered, bleeding body of Jesus on the cross next to him. He knew Jesus was the sovereign of this situation as of all other situations. He knew Jesus was going to "come into his kingdom" and humbly asked to be included when it all happened. The King granted that wish. While the sky went black, the earth's crust rumbled in agony, and the graves opened to proclaim the victory, Jesus and the thief walked together into the throne room of the Father as co-heirs of the kingdom. Even a dying thief can possess a kingdom mentality by recognizing the sovereignty of Christ.

The Growing Establishment

Deep within the psychological makeup of every person is a desire to be on "the winning side." Propaganda experts call it a "bandwagon" psychology because they know how rapidly you can create a crowd and start a parade if you just create a lot of hoopla. People start thinking "something big is happening and I'll really miss out if I don't follow along."

Has the church ever missed out on this one! As I think back on the Christians I have known, I don't think two percent communicated to me that the cause of Christ was a-building and that anyone that missed out would miss life's greatest adventure. I haven't seen a bandwagon psychology; it has been a funeral procession psychology. It didn't excite me at all that I could spend a lifetime serving the Master. In fact, making a million bucks selling life insurance would have been just as satisfying. At many key decision points "following through" in obedience to Christ was motivated by a sense of *duty* rather than a sense of *adventure*. It "would be worth it all when I saw Jesus." Until then it would be a living death!

I am told that at certain points during World War II, one of America's few "popular" wars, volunteers stood in line to enlist because they felt that the cause was worthwhile and it was the thing every patriotic young man should do. The building of the kingdom of Jesus Christ was never made to me a popular struggle, an adventure to which the most outstanding young man or woman would gladly give himself. Quite the contrary. I got the image that the missionary was an obsolete, mediocre person who "sacrificed" greatly—a person for whom you had a certain spiritual respect but for whom you also felt sorry.

I had to struggle with God's call on my life as a young collegian. I knew his call was real and my obligation was equally real. But I struggled with "following through" because the other options open to a young man were communicated to be so much more attractive. I actually sought entrance to law school to enter politics because my life as a Christian servant seemed, from that vantage point, to be so dull by comparison. I've had a little taste of politics since then, and I know from experience that no adventure in the world exceeds the one of being involved in the growing establishment of the kingdom of Jesus Christ!

No one ever adopts a kingdom mentality unless he comes to an unshakable commitment that the sovereign Christ is building his kingdom *now*! At this point one's doctrine is critically important. Some systems of doctrine virtually guarantee that a person is not going to be involved in the building of the kingdom. Some doctrines that assure this are:

1. The kingdom is future; it is a one-thousand-year rule of Christ that has not begun.
2. The kingdom is past; it was offered to Israel and, when Israel refused it, it was gone.
3. The kingdom is just spiritual; it is a mystical rule of Christ in the hearts of believers.

4. The kingdom is socio-political; we must build the kingdom by changing the social or political order.

The ironic thing about all of these doctrines is that they possess elements of truth or are completely true when placed in perspective:

1. The kingdom *is* future, a one-thousand-year rule of Christ on earth (Revelation 20:4-5).
2. The kingdom *was* offered to Israel and Israel refused it (Matthew 21:43).
3. The kingdom *is* spiritual, an enthronement of Christ in our hearts (Romans 14:17-18).
4. The kingdom *is* socio-political (Revelation 11:15-18).

But to limit the concept of the kingdom to any one of the above dimensions destroys its vitality and relegates the concept to a nice theological construct, little more.

The kingdom must be defined as:

> God's eternal plan to destroy his enemies, liberate mankind from their grasp, and establish his rule upon the earth through his Son, Jesus Christ.

This definition encompasses God's activity from Genesis to Revelation, from the fall of Satan to his eternal judgment, from the initial plan for atonement to its fruition in the day of Christ's revelation. It tells us that the establishment of the kingdom is an ongoing process. It is not all in the past, nor all in the future. It is present tense!

Invincible and Perfect

I get goosebumps just thinking of the lines from Handel's "Hallelujah Chorus" (based on Revelation 11:15 and other passages) which proclaim, "And He shall reign forever and ever, King of Kings and Lord of Lords. . . ." I think back of the tear-stained cheeks I have observed at the end of Handel's "Messiah", whole audiences of believers bursting to their feet to join in the exaltation of Jesus of Nazareth. I think that for a few moments those believers have caught sight of the invincibility of Jesus Christ and his cause. As much as my country's national anthem stirs me, it does nothing compared to the "Hallelujah Chorus." Why? My nation, as great as its past, present or future glories may be, will fade, collapse and die. But the kingdom to which I am committed will never die, will never fade, will never be conquered throughout all the eons of eternity. It is invincible.

The Apostle Paul saw this great invincibility when he said:

> Then the end will come, when he hands over the kingdom to God the Father after he has destroyed all dominion, authority, and power. For he must reign until God has put all his enemies under his feet. The last enemy to be destroyed is death. (1 Corinthians 15:24-26 NIV).

But not only is the kingdom of Jesus Christ invincible, it is *perfect*! Its perfection must embarrass the Utopian thinkers of the past. I grew up in Indiana and in that state a group of Utopian thinkers established a small community called "New Harmony." They foresaw a community in which a new and special kind of human coalition could be built. The ruins of that "perfect society" remain today. They are mute testimony that until Jesus of Nazareth produces a "new harmony" in a world order of his own, all human "new harmonies" will be discordant melodies based on the same old themes.

Not so the kingdom. Listen to the state of things in the kingdom of Jesus Christ as described by the Apostle John in the Book of Revelation:

> Therefore, they are before the throne of God and serve him day and night in his temple; and he who sits on the throne will spread his tent over them. Never again will

they hunger; never again will they thirst. The sun will not beat upon them, nor any scorching heat. For the Lamb at the center of the throne will be their shepherd; he will lead them to springs of living water. And God will wipe away every tear from their eyes (Revelation 7:15-17 NIV).

Blush, Utopians, blush! Wince, Marxists, wince! Your perfect societies are nothing compared to the society of the King! In his perfect kingdom there is:

no fear - the King's tent of protection covers,
no danger - the King's tent of protection covers,
no hunger - the King provides food,
no thirst - the King provides drink,
no uncomfortable temperatures - the King controls the thermostat on the universe,
no lack of guidance - the King will act as a shepherd,
no sorrow or pain - the King will wipe away all tears.

No one can make the kind of commitment that the kingdom of Jesus Christ demands of its subjects unless that person is convinced that the sacrifice will result in something far superior to that of human solutions. It is far easier to surrender to the King when you realize that his kingdom is both *invincible* and *perfect*.

A World Order

Finally, the kingdom of Jesus Christ is a world order. It is relevant to this whirling sphere and its creatures. It is total and not partial. It leaves no pockets of unconquered guerillas in the mountains. It is the ultimate and complete conquest of all alien forces *on this globe* and the establishment of a literal, political rule *on this globe*.

The word used in the Greek New Testament most often for this world is the word *kosmos*. It is the word from which we get our English word "cosmetics." The link between these two apparently diverse concepts, "world" and "cosmetics," lies in the connotation of the word *kosmos*. It indicates the "system" or "arrangement" of things. When a woman wants to change the "arrangement" of her face (eyebrows higher, lips broader, cheeks rosier) she uses "cosmetics." When the King wants to make an impact on the world, he isn't going to waste his time on the superficial dimensions. He is going to change the entire order, arrangement, system—the very molecular structure—of the world. He is going to introduce a new *world order*.

Man will live in perfect brotherhood. There will be no market for military armaments, because people will be "beating their swords into plowshares and their spears into pruning hooks" (Isaiah 2:4). Imagine the audacity of the United Nations placing that verse, a messianic verse, a kingdom verse, on the U.N. Building. What a slap at the King even to intimate that a new world order could be ushered in by a measly assembly of world leaders who can't even agree at the table, much less in political action. More plowshares have been beat into swords and more pruning hooks have been made into spears since the beginning of the United Nations than at any other time in human history.

But the King will fashion and *is now fashioning* a new world order in which

> The kingdom of the world has become the kingdom of
> our Lord and of His Christ, and he will reign forever
> and ever (Revelation 11:15b NIV).

The entrance to this new world of the kingdom, the gate to conquest, is commitment—a commitment to Jesus Christ that results in new birth and citizenship in the kingdom, and a commitment that espouses his plan to establish an invincible and perfect world order. I challenge you,

ENTER THE GATE! ENTER THE GATE!

6 The Kingdom Lifestyle

A few months ago I was in a store that sold novelty items and was looking through some of the humorous signs they were selling. There was the usual collection of somewhat familiar "You don't have to be crazy to work here, but it helps" signs, a few others which were new to me, and one that hit me hard:

THE GOLDEN RULE: THEM THAT HAS THE GOLD MAKES THE RULES.

As I reflected on the underlying philosophy of the sign, it began to speak to me something that affects our thinking here.

First of all, it is obvious that the sign was a takeoff on the teaching of Jesus that we should do unto others as we would have them do unto us, the "golden rule." This principle is mouthed as a "guiding ethic" by many people who do not even profess faith in Jesus Christ. It is a high standard for human relationships. But the humor in the sign I saw was tied to the cynical observation that the golden rule is not what is really practiced. In practice those with power (wealth) make the rules for others, I presume in their own self interest.

This sign was making a statement that the ethic of Jesus is not the ethic of the world system. They are entirely different. I agree. The world cannot even approach the ethic of Jesus. The ethic of Jesus is so high that not even Christians can attain it. Living a truly "Christian" life is not difficult, it is *impossible*. For the ethic of Jesus is the supernatural ethic—it is the ethic of the kingdom, a kingdom lifestyle.

In fact, the kingdom of this world is diametrically opposed to the kingdom of Jesus Christ. If the kingdom ethic of Jesus Christ is the *system*, then the ethic of the world is an *anti-system*. This is true to such an extent that Bill Gothard, the well known American Bible teacher, observed that he could make a simple test to discover how God would think and respond to any given situation. First, he said, he would analyze his "most natural response" to any situation. Then he would ask himself, "what is the exact opposite of my natural response?" He discovered that more often than not the *opposite* was quite in line with the teaching of Jesus, the precepts of Scripture.

Nowhere is this more graphically illustrated than in the teaching of Jesus on a kingdom lifestyle, the "Sermon on the Mount." When Jesus finished this message on the quality of life and ethics which were the mark of his character, the world system stood forever condemned. For not one person on the earth can live up to these standards in his own strength. They are supernatural, impossible, kingdom standards. Let's examine a few and see.

The first thing Jesus did was set forth a list of character traits which he viewed as acceptable, honorable, "blessed." In this first step he set himself at odds with the world system. He put his stamp of approval on the

poor in spirit
mourning
meek
starved for righteousness
merciful
pure in heart
peacemakers
persecuted for righteousness, and
insulted for being Christ's.

Now let me ask, "Are these the values that cause the world system to exalt a man?" Hardly. How many people ever got into *Who's Who* for being meek and for hungering and thirsting after righteousness? How many were ever elected mayor or president of the Rotary Club because they were poor in spirit and pure in heart? I mean *really* pure in heart.

I got involved in what became an international controversy one time by challenging the standards of purity of the secular society. When Apollo 10 astronauts peppered their communications with ground control with four-letter words, blasphemies, and references to sexual intercourse, I expressed my objection to NASA in a telegram. When the press picked up the story, I became the butt of an incredible attack which included threats, denunciations, and even a decision by a major city newspaper columnist to make me "Prude of the Year." The world ethic doesn't mind a *little* purity, but it is grossly intolerant of any standard that rises too far above or sinks too far below its own.

But if Jesus got away from the world's value system by a listing of the personal character traits he honors, he really "blew it" with the rest of the talk! He went so far as to proclaim:

1. If Christians don't make an impact on the secular society (salt and light), they are worthless.
2. If anyone breaks even the tiniest part of his law, he will be "least in the kingdom."
3. Nobody can enter the kingdom unless his righteousness exceeds that of the religious *leaders*.
4. Hate is as much sin as murder.
5. Lust is as much sin as adultery.
6. Quick settlement of differences is the only way to avoid judgment.
7. Cutting off a hand is preferable to letting that hand cause you to sin.

8. Swearing an oath by anything is wrong; your word ought to be law without oaths.

If there was anyone left by that point in the message, they packed up their duds on the following remarks:

1. Do not resist an evil person; if he strikes you on one cheek, offer the other.
2. If someone sues you for your coat, offer to *give* him your overcoat.
3. If someone *forces* you to go one mile, volunteer to go a second mile.
4. Give to anyone asking you for help.
5. Don't avoid a person who wants to borrow from you; lend to him and don't expect repayment.
6. If someone steals from you, don't ask for your goods back.
7. Love, pray for, and do good to your enemies.

Now if you got through the last list without saying, "Oh, come on now, that's *ridiculous!*" then you either didn't understand those standards or you are already committed to a kingdom lifestyle. Which was it?

I was a Christian for nearly eighteen years before I realized that unless I lived up to *these* standards, I would not impress God a bit with my morality. I was a Christian twenty years before I refused to ask for money back that was stolen from me. And I called myself a Christian! I certainly was not a kingdom Christian. I did not espouse the ethic of the kingdom.

E. Stanley Jones illustrates the kingdom lifestyle in the story of a man who bought a house and shortly thereafter began to erect a fence between his property and his neighbor's. As he began the fence, his neighbor came storming out to confront him with the words, "Listen, buddy, when you bought the house, you bought a lawsuit. You erect that fence there and it will be five feet onto my property." The

Christian replied, "I knew I would always have good relationships with my neighbors. That is very important to me. I'll tell you what, you erect the fence where it should go and send me the bill." The fence was never erected. The ethic of the kingdom prevailed.

As soon as I got serious about adopting a kingdom lifestyle and ethic, God began to test my resolve. His first lesson was to love an enemy. I had a fiery, red-haired neighbor who was one of the most ill-tempered men I've known. He let it be known to me and others that he hated religious people. I happened to fit his definition of "religious people." One day he and another neighbor and I were standing on the corner of my lot talking. He told a filthy joke and then looked at me and, in his most biting, sarcastic tones, said, "Oh, excuse me, Reverend." I walked away from that Saturday morning encounter really "steamed up."

I began to hear the voice of God speaking to me in my heart. "You hypocrite, you preach love, but you don't love this neighbor." I argued a bit with God about what a vile, ill-tempered man he was, but God didn't buy my arguments so I capitulated. "God," I said, "I can't love that man, but I know that you can. Please control me and create love for him through me. Thank you, Father, I believe you will."

A few weeks later there was a reenactment of the original scene on a Saturday morning on the corner of my lawn with the same two neighbors. My antagonist was in rare form that morning. He was damning the waste pickup division of our county because they had been erratic in their service. He was damning the ethnic group that predominated in that division. The air was blue with expostulations when I had the strangest sensation. I wanted to put my arms around the man and tell him I loved him (not choke him to death!). For the first time I saw him as a troubled and needy person and the object of God's love.

Our whole relationship changed after that. The kingdom ethic prevailed.

It wasn't long after that God gave me another lesson in kingdom ethics. One of my employees, a Christian, mounted a well-organized and highly effective attack on my character among the staff of the college where I was president. It was a covert attack, so for weeks I didn't know what was going on. But I began to sense that some of my most trusted and faithful co-workers were getting increasingly distant in their relationships with me. One Christian brother who had been a friend since high school days couldn't look me in the eye.

I asked God for direction, and in a staff meeting one day said that I sensed that there was tension in our relationships and a wrong spirit. I suggested that if I had done anything to offend, they owed it to me to tell me so that I could make things right. Within twenty-four hours I got two epistles, one from the attacker and one from his closest co-worker. The letter from the attacker was a number of pages long and had ten or twelve charges which accused me of not being willing to deal with certain issues with the faculty publicly. It accused me of keeping information regarding some staff problems from the board of trustees and lying about my personal finances at a time when the faculty and staff were hurting due to delayed paychecks.

My first thought was to fire the individual. The charges were so malicious and untrue that I would have been "justified" in so doing—by the "world ethic," that is. God impressed the kingdom ethic on me and insisted that I do the following:

1. Love the man;
2. Sit down with him and ask him what *he* would like me to do to respond to his charges;
3. Do what he said.

We spent about three hours together going over the dozen or so charges. He dared me to present certain issues to the faculty. I called a special meeting with those items as the only agenda items. He dared me to let a faculty person appear before the board of trustees. I arranged with the board to allow *him* to appear before them and volunteered to stay out of the meeting so that there would be no lack of freedom for him to speak. Since he had questioned my personal finances, I disclosed them to him. I offered to share my income tax returns and other personal financial data both with him and with the faculty and staff. The problem was over in forty-eight hours. The kingdom ethic had prevailed.

Since then I have had numerous other opportunities to employ the kingdom ethic, to adopt for myself and for my family a kingdom lifestyle. I went to bat for a Christian brother who had been fired from a Christian college and wanted to return to Christian service. I interceded for him with my board of trustees, hired him, and loaned him one thousand dollars to help make the downpayment on a new house. He changed his mind about the job a week or two before the start of the school year. He broke his contract, and , when he could not get his house deposit back, refused to repay the loan. When I wrote to him with strong counsel about the wrong that he did, he cut off all communication and returned subsequent letters unopened, "refused" through the postal system.

Over the years I have had the joy of praying for that dear brother and his wife. When I pass through his city, I always think of him and pray that God will deal lovingly and mercifully with him. I have even hoped on occasion that he never does pay back the note. The joy I have had trusting the King with this situation is too great to be spoiled by having the money repaid. What a thrill to live a kingdom lifestyle!

You see, it would have been foolish for Jesus to have set forth a system that was a rehash, a warm over, a regurgitation of the world ethic. Anyone, even those not a part of his kingdom, could have achieved the standards through self effort and self righteousness without ever establishing an intimate relationship with the King. If Jesus had done this, he would have launched another world religion. He had no such intention. The world was already groaning under the yoke of world religions. He came to offer citizenship in a *supernatural* system, not a natural one. He came to offer the kingdom of heaven to earth so that it could be the kingdom of earth. We have consistently rejected the kingdom and have made a world religion out of Christianity—a hated world religion at that.

In Guatemala I saw painted on the two-story wall of a dormitory at the University the symbol of Christ, the Greek leters chi and rho (X and P) fashioned into a sword and plunged into a map of Guatemala. Blood gushed from the wound. There was no need for a caption. Christianity was bleeding the country; that was the message. Maybe the Christian *religion* was bleeding the country, but the *kingdom* of Jesus Christ was not! Maybe the *human system* was bleeding their fatherland, but *God's system* wasn't! Maybe the *lifestyle of the church* was killing their nation, but the *kingdom lifestyle* wasn't! The principles of the Sermon on the Mount liberate. The principles of the kingdom of darkness enslave.

How do your propose to respond to what I am saying? Are you going to make up a list of resolutions to abide by the standards of the Sermon on the Mount? Do you intend to "become more active in church" so that you can begin to live a kingdom lifestyle? Are you planning to make a new commitment to Jesus Christ so that from that decision you can "flesh out" the kingdom ethic? Are you going to vow to read your Bible five minutes every day so that this biblical input will produce the qualities of a citizen of the kingdom in you? Forget all such proposals. They will not work!!

I have been keeping from you the most significant concept God ever gave for beginning a kingdom lifestyle. Did you ever wonder why the Old Testament doesn't include pictures of the kingdom lifestyle lived out by the believers? Ever wonder why the Sermon on the Mount wasn't given at Sinai? I'll tell you why. Grace. God knew we could never elevate our standards to the level he had revealed. No need putting us under the pile of even loftier ones.

But he knew something else. He knew that only he with his infinite moral perfection could attain these standards. There was no use laying a divine expectation on a human shoulder or placing an infinite requirement on finite creatures. After all he *had* tried:

1. He had judged Adam and Eve and sent them from the Garden to indicate his perspective on sin;
2. He had destroyed the wicked population in a universal inundation to emphasize his standards;
3. He had provided patriarchal leadership to produce righteousness.
4. He provided a complete cataloguing of his standards in the Mosaic law to provide moral guidelines;
5. He provided a continuing series of divinely appointed spokesmen called prophets to give ongoing insight into righteousness;
6. He established a theocracy and later a divinely anointed king to lead the people into his way;
7. He provided a living example of the kind of life he wanted man to live by taking on flesh himself!

All of the above failed to produce a kingdom lifestyle in believers. The church today has "demythologized the fall," debunked the flood story, ridiculed the patriarchs and prophets, used the Mosaic Law to produce religious cults and isms that ignore Christ, and suggested that the life of Jesus was a fraud, a fake, or, in part, a "Passover plot."

Obviously, after all of that, the only solution would be one in which *God himself* could live out these standards in the lives of his followers. Only then could the principles of the kingdom of heaven be worked out in the midst of the kingdom of this world. That would be the GENIUS SOLUTION.

Why, if this solution were ever effected, there would not be a single citizen of the kingdom that could not see that kingdom lifestyle produced in his life. *God himself* would produce it in and through him. God living like God in man, his infinite Spirit motivating, empowering and guiding every kingdom citizen who is surrendered to his sovereignty. An incredibly exciting concept! A dynamite idea!

That is exactly what God put into operation. It it called the Spirit-controlled life. Some refer to it as the Spirit-filled life, the abundant life or sanctification, the effects of the second blessing. It doesn't matter what you call it so long as you recognize it to be *God living in his born-again child.* God wants to produce his character in us. That is the kingdom life. That produces a kingdom lifestyle.

How I wish I had discovered the Spirit-controlled life years before I did. For eighteen years I struggled to produce a kingdom lifestyle on my own. I sought to produce supernatural fruit on my vine through obedience or faithfulness or sincerity. I tried to live like Jesus without the control of the Spirit of Jesus. My witness was ineffective (five people trusting Christ through it in eighteen years!). My fruit, when you examined it closely, said "made in occupied Poland." My life was a giant roller coaster speeding through slump after slump to "rededications" of my life to

Christ. An extended exercise in frustration. A child of the kingdom living like a faithful member of the Christian world religion. Born to fly and hopping on the ground.

No wonder Jesus told his followers that it would be better for them if he went away, because if he did not go away the Divine Companion would not come to be in them (John 16:6-7). He knew that the indwelling Spirit ("He lives *with* you and will be *in* you"—John 14:17b NIV) would make all the difference in the world.

If you wondered how Larry Poland could respond like that to a hateful neighbor, an attacking employee and an ungrateful Christian friend, you just found out. Larry Poland couldn't. Only God could, and it was the empowering of the Christ that indwells Larry Poland that made those responses possible.

Maybe you picked it up in my narration of the struggle to love my hateful neighbor. I prayed, "God, I can't love that man, but I know you can. Please *control me* and *create love* for him *through me*." That was the secret. I was allowing the King to produce a royal response in a commoner.

One final example. A businessman in the office equipment business was referred to me as a Christian philanthropist who was interested in helping Christian colleges financially. Since I was the president of a Christian college, I was interested. I made arrangements for him to visit our campus. I rolled out the red carpet, cleared my schedule for a couple of days, and shared with him the vision, program and needs of our school. He was impressed. He talked of contributing cash and equipment in the range of $100,000 to $200,000. I was still interested!

He left the campus and returned a few weeks later with the first installment on his gifts, a beautiful, reconditioned automatic typewriter that would reproduce preprogramed content automatically with speed and accuracy. The campus buzzed with the goodness of God in sending this generous Christian businessmen to help our school. Other gifts followed. He provided skilled labor for the completion of one wing of a new building. He talked of acquiring a $200,000 computer for us. We were overjoyed.

We had been trying to get some videotape equipment for some time and I inquired whether he could acquire it for us at a good price. He assured me that he could get it for us at the wholesale price and that he would be happy to donate part of it. Since I had been setting aside some of my giving to the Lord's work for this project, I contributed $1,000 to the cost of the equipment. He returned to his home (about 1300 miles away) and we waited with anticipation for the next contributions to arrive.

A week or so had passed when I received a call from an irate gentlemen asking why we had not "made good" on the $10,000 check we had written to the businessman. I responded there must be some misunderstanding, that our school had not written any such check. He responded that the "philanthropist" had written him a check that had bounced. When confronted, the businessman said we had written him a bogus check which had caused his check to the caller to bounce in turn. I explained that such was not the case and terminated the call cordially.

But now I began to wonder. I called a friend in another college that had been a recipient of gifts from the businessman—reportedly some $40,000 worth. He responded, "Walt got you, too? Oh, no. Some of the things he gave us, he did not own. We have been tracking true owners and we're informed that there are thirteen warrants out for his arrest." My heart sank. Walt (not his real name) was a crook. I pictured my $1,000 flying out the window.

The next few days were misery. I schemed how I could get that $1,000 back. I plotted vengeance. After all, I reasoned, that was not *my* money; that was God's! Apparently God did not need my help, for he began to talk to me about some "kingdom principles." He reminded me what Jesus said about not asking for the return of stolen property. I winced.

Finally, after a few days of inner struggle, I capitulated to the kingdom principle. I confessed to God that I was not capable of loving or forgiving the man and "writing off" the $1,000. I asked his indwelling Spirit to control me and to produce those kingdom responses. I sat down to write the most ridiculous letter of my life.

"Dear Walt," I wrote, "I know now that your intentions were not honorable in the acceptance of the $1,000 for the video equipment, and I have heard that you are being sought for a number of other offenses. I think you need to know the seriousness of the things you have done and that God will deal justly with you."

"My purpose for writing, however, is that I want you to know that I have forgiven you and that if you ever have any need that I can meet, I stand ready to serve you as a brother in Christ."

A long time later I was sitting in my office when my secretary buzzed me and said, "You'll never believe who's here. Walt!" I asked her to send him in and he came through my door looking like a defeated man. "Walt," I said, "what brings you here?" "I came to make things right," he replied. "Walt, maybe you didn't understand my letter. You don't have to make anything right. It's all forgiven."

"I had to come back, Larry," he said. "God hasn't let me rest since I got your letter. I know I have done a lot of things wrong to a lot of people, mostly Christians. But none of them responded like you did, and I haven't been able to forget it. I've brought you this new electronic calculator to make things right."

"Is it paid for?" I asked. When he assured me that it was, I accepted it on behalf of the school. He owed me nothing.

I've thought many, many times what kind of impact the Church could have on a unbelieving world if every citizen of the kingdom operated in the power of the Spirit according to kingdom principles even for six weeks. The world then would "see our good works and glorify our Father who is in heaven." The vitality of the Church would be enhanced a thousand fold. The impact of kingdom principles would cause millions to desire to be part of a system in which such principles were applied. They would stand in line to learn how they too could be part of the kingdom of Jesus Christ.

It is a curse for a Christian to be indistinguishable from good moral unbelievers. The Christian is designed to live on the supernatural principles of the kingdom and he is empowered to do so. If he doesn't, he doesn't deserve to bear the name "Christian." He doesn't deserve to carry the banner of the kingdom. He doesn't have a *kingdom* lifestyle.

Living according to the kingdom principles in the power of the Holy Spirit transports us into the same quality of life that will predominate throughout the eternal kingdom of Jesus Christ. When the Pharisees accused Jesus of casting out demons "by Beelzebub, the prince of demons," Jesus responded:

> And if I drive out demons by Beelzebub, by whom do your people drive them out? So then they will be your judges. But if I drive out demons by the Spirit of God, then the kingdom of God has come upon you (Matthew 12:27-28 NIV).

When a mortal operates under the power of the Spirit of God, then the kingdom has come upon him. If every human being operated under the power of the Spirit of God, the kingdom of Jesus Christ would, by definition, be established.

In Matthew 16:18-19, Jesus promised to give to Peter the "keys to the kingdom." These keys would be used to open up the power of God to his body of believers to the extent that even the gates of hell would not be able to hold out against its attack. With the indwelling Christ empowering each individual in the Church and the indwelling Spirit guiding each step, the believer could "bind things on earth and have them bound in heaven." He could "loose things on earth and have them loosed in heaven." At that point the kingdom of heaven and the world system would intersect through the meeting of human and divine. This would produce a heavenly lifestyle in the midst of the kingdom of this world.

How criminal that some have taken this glorious concept and have tied Peter and the "keys" to an earthly, ecclesiastical system and not the kingdom of God. Little wonder that that ecclesiastical system, as all other ecclesiastical systems, has failed to produce the lifestyle of the King—the kingdom lifestyle.

If you have never experienced the coming of the kingdom of God upon you producing kingdom responses, and a kingdom lifestyle, stop reading right here, confess all known sin, and ask the Spirit of God to control you. Thank him by faith for so doing and take one "giant step" into the kingdom.

7 Kingdom Citizenship

My passport is filled with stamps of various governments into whose realms I have traveled. These indicate that I have been the recipient of governmental privilege, the privilege of visiting, doing business or just passing through territory under the authority of that government. Setting foot in another governmental realm not only gives me the opportunity to make use of the privileges, but also puts me under the restraints and restrictions of that government. For instance, I have visited countries that were under curfew. I was under curfew. Even though I was not a citizen of that nation, I was under curfew. Interestingly enough, though, I was still under the constraints of the country in which I hold citizenship. I was not able to vote or join the armed forces of the host country or *my* country would take my citizenship away.

This is much the case with citizenship in the kingdom of Jesus Christ. Joining the kingdom of Jesus Christ revokes our citizenship in the kingdom of this world, even though we continue to live as aliens in it for the remainder of our physical lives. This creates a "dynamic tension" between the expectations of our heavenly kingdom and the earthly ones in which we reside as aliens. Jesus could not have been more clear in establishing this fact.

In John 18:36 Jesus was being grilled by Pilate on the charge that he was the monarch of a kingdom in opposition to the authority of Rome. Pilate asked Jesus if he was the king of the Jews. Jesus responded that his kingdom was not of this world and that if it were, "then his servants would *fight*" to prevent his arrest by the Jews. Jesus had shortly before directed Peter to put his sword back into its sheath, but not before Peter had cut off Malchus's ear. Jesus knew that his kingdom was not to be established by the methods of the earthly kingdoms which focus on violent self-defense without respect for the authority of God.

On another occasion Jesus was being attacked by those who were seeking to exploit his teaching of the "other kingdom" by pitting it clearly against the authority of Rome. Jesus surprised them and foiled the attempt by calling for a coin. Pointing out that the coin had the picture of Caesar on it, he directed them to "render to Caesar the things due Caesar." He made sure they understood, additionally, that they were not to neglect "rendering to God the things due him" (Matthew 21:22). In so doing, Jesus focused on a dilemma which rests with us today. When these two lines of authority, *human government* and *heavenly government*, come into conflict, how is it to be resolved? How can we, in our most conscientious endeavors to submit to the authorities over us, avoid serving one kingdom and offending the other?

At this point rests the genius of kingdom citizenship. The solution to this dilemma is rooted in the whole concept of the privileges and expectations of kingdom citizenship and the standards placed on those who are part of the kingdom of Jesus Christ.

It *is* clear that change of citizenship has already been effected for those who are born again. It is not something which we await. The Apostle Paul stated this emphatically in his letter to the Colossians. He said, "For he (God) has rescued us from the dominion of darkness and brought us into the kingdom of the Son he loves, in whom we have redemption, the forgiveness of sins" (Colossians 1:13-14 NIV). One version says that we have been "translated" into the kingdom of Christ. But it is clear that the shift in citizenship is *past tense* for those who have capitulated to the King.

It is also clear that kingdom citizenship creates immense privileges for the one possessing it. It provides the continuous, unbroken presence of the King and the implicatiohs of his absolute authority in every contingency of life. Matthew 28:18 speaks of the total authority of Jesus over all creation. We also have the promise that he will never leave or forsake his followers. These ideas support the concept that a citizen of the kingdom of Jesus Christ possesses all the authority of the universe.

In ancient civilizations, the vizier or prime minister to the monarch was often given custody of the signet ring of the king or pharoah. With this ring came the full authority of the king to transact business and enforce decrees. Both Daniel and Joseph in the Old Testament were granted this privilege. In like manner, the citizen of the kingdom of Jesus Christ is given the *seal* of the indwelling Holy Spirit (Ephesians 1:13). He is thus authorized to transact eternal business with the full confidence that no authority figure in heaven or on earth will be able to overrule, recind or ignore the decrees made with this seal. An unspeakable privilege, don't you agree, for a mortal to make "binding and loosing" commitments with the full force of deity?

But the translation from the government of this world into citizenship of the kingdom of Jesus Christ is only part of the privilege. It was not enough for him just to create "naturalized" citizens. He made sure that they were actually *reborn* into the kingdom. There was no such thing as citizens by birth and citizens by naturalization—all were citizens by birth. This rebirth, then, not only consummated our union to the kingdom but (in an incredible act of grace on the part of the King) also brought us into the *royal family*! Thus, in one act we became citizens of the kingdom and children of the Monarch, part of the nobility that rules the kingdom! And, if *this* were not enough, we were written into the royal will as equal heirs and heiresses of the royal fortune! Isn't this the import of Paul's teaching in Romans 1:15-17?

> For you did not receive a spirit that makes you a slave again to fear, but you received the Spirit who makes you sons. And by him we cry, "Abba, Father." The Spirit himself testifies with our spirit that we are God's children. Now if we are God's children, then we are heirs—heirs of God and co-heirs with Christ, if indeed we share in his sufferings in order that we may also share in his glory (NIV).

The King's presence, kingdom authority, rebirth into the royal family, entrance into the royal will—these still don't begin to exhaust the privileges of kingdom citizenship! We have the privilege of drawing *immediately*, not just through a future inheritance, on the treasures of the kingdom. Jesus taught that one who had been instructed about the kingdom is like the owner of a house who "brings out of his storeroom new treasures as well as old" (Matthew 13:52 NIV). Every member of the royal family has the privilege of drawing on the resources of the royal treasury. We have these treasures to *share* with others, not to hoard for ourselves. We are promised the supply of all of our needs "according to his glorious riches" (Philippians 4:19 NIV).

Another kingdom privilege is the priestly office which we assume when we are citizens. Many political systems of the past and present have been dominated by the religious leaders of the society. This was true in ancient Egypt, in many Eastern civilizations and is true in many parts of the world today. The King of kings was not going to deprive us of such privilege.

So he has made us a "royal priesthood" according to

1 Peter 2:9; a "kingdom of priests" according to the Apostle John in Revelation 5:10.

We dare not take lightly the role of priestly intercessor. It is critical to the plan of the King for the building of his kingdom. You see, once we have been born into the kingdom of Jesus Christ, we become divinely appointed agents of the king to extend the boundaries of the kingdom to those in darkness. We become the ones who have the privilege of interceding on behalf of the lost with the High Priest. The High Priest is the only mediator with God the Father (1 Timothy 2:5), but we become "mediators" carrying the message of the Good News of the Kingdom to those who are not aware of it or who have not yet accepted it. "How shall they hear without a preacher?" Paul asks in Romans in 10:14 (KJV).

Examples of this priestly intercession by believers are plentiful. Unbelieving homes are said to be "sanctified" by the presence of one member of the kingdom (1 Corinthians 7:14). We are "agents of reconciliation" used by God to reconcile a lost world to himself (2 Corinthians 5:18-19). In Ephesians 6:10-18 where we are given the "whole armor of God," we are told to "take the helmet of salvation". This has great relevance to this priestly role we play.

In the ancient Roman army, which provides the context for Paul's description of the armor, you could instantly tell the rank and division of a soldier by his helmet. Plumage, style, shape, material and insignia all marked the helmet of the Roman soldier. I personally feel that Paul was pointing indirectly to the priestly role we are to play in a lost world, in the spiritual war, by exhorting us to take the helmet of salvation. Every citizen of the kingdom should be instantly recognizable because his helmet, the most prominent and visible part of his armor, says to all, *"Salvation!"* Everywhere the kingdom citizen goes he should be shouting to all, "I am identified with *Salvation!"*

One group of believers distributed bumper stickers

that said, *"It's Fun Being Saved."* That is a contemporary medium for communicating the helmet of salvation concept. If some enslaved member of the kingdom of darkness wanted to enter the kingdom of Jesus Christ, would he immediately come to *you* because *you* are wearing the helmet of salvation in the community, because *you* are exercising the priestly intercession privilege, because *you* are the one through whom others are entering the kingdom regularly?

Last week I stepped into a used furniture store to inquire about an antique clock that was displayed for sale. After I purchased the clock, I told the shop owner that I would like to share with him a little booklet that described how he could have a personal relationship with God through Jesus Christ. He responded, "Boy, do I ever need that!" I explained the plan of salvation and asked him if he would like to invite Jesus Christ to be his personal Savior and Lord. He replied, "I sure would," That man was reconciled to God through the priestly mediation of a citizen of the kingdom.

The overwhelmingly wonderful, excitingly fabulous, abundantly extravagant privileges of citizenship in the kingdom! It is unbelievable, but true, that many citizens of the kingdom never exercise the authority, build on the family relationship, draw on the royal treasury or exercise the priestly office that is theirs. They live as *practical* citizens of the kingdom of darkness while they are *actual* citizens of the kingdom of heaven.

This reminds me of the time I was the guest of others at a lovely and expensive hotel in Latin America. The hotel had an internationally honored restaurant, exquisite accommodations and a beautiful patio with formal gardens, exotic tropical birds and breathtaking flowers. For a number of days I enjoyed the privileges of a guest at the hotel, with one exception. The first day I was there, I discovered another section of the formal gardens which had a beautiful swimming pool, expensive statuary, more exotic birds and beautiful flowers. It was far more beautiful than the garden in which I had spent most of my relaxing hours. But it was separated from the main garden by an iron gate which was locked.

I observed that even though many people came to sit in the gardens and sip cool tropical drinks, none ventured beyond the locked door into the most beautiful area of all. Only once or twice did I see a handful of people behind that locked gate. I assumed that they had gained entrance through some other gate or were "privileged characters" of some kind, perhaps the owners of the hotel.

My stay at the hotel came to an end. I packed my things, delivered them to the lobby, and decided to take one last look around the beautiful grounds before my friend came to take me to the airport. As I was about to turn in my room key I took one last, longing look through the iron gate. I looked at the key and noticed another key on the ring, a smaller one. I wondered what it was for when it occurred to me to try it in the lock on the garden gate.

When I tried the key, it opened the iron gate easily. It was obviously made for that lock! For days I had held in my pocket the key to that gorgeous pool and garden. It was reserved for the guests of the hotel and was locked to the casual visitor who might come to the restaurant for food or drink. *I* was the "privileged person" for whom that area was reserved! I failed to exercise that privilege merely because I never turned the key. I spent only fifteen minutes in an area that was held in reserve for me for the entirety of my stay. The story of the kingdom citizen that never exercises the privileges of kingdom citizenship!

There is another privilege which citizens of the kingdom enjoy. It is access to the innermost secrets of the King. In Matthew 13 Jesus told his disciples that, "The knowledge of the secrets of the kingdom of heaven has been given to you but not to them," i.e., unbelievers. He explained this to justify his repeated teaching in parables which the unbelievers did not understand and which had to be explained in private even to the disciples. This same concept is set forth in 1 Corinthians 2 by the Apostle Paul as he declares that the wisdom to which we are party is not possessed by the rulers of this age. It is "hidden wisdom" that God has destined for our glory before the worlds began. Paul explains that this wisdom is "foolishness" to the man without the Spirit and that he cannot understand spiritual principles because they are spiritually discerned. The kingdom citizen, on the contrary, understands the "deep things of God" through the Spirit that indwells him and has access to the deep, inner recesses of the mind of God. This is the ultimate privilege of the kingdom ingroup. A popular musical contains a song line, "I wonder what the king is thinking tonight?" the expression of a commoner who wishes he could probe the thoughts of the monarch. The citizen of the kingdom of Jesus Christ is given access to all of the classified, top secret, inner workings of the King's mind.

It may well be due to failure to exercise this last privilege that more do not enter the kingdom or, as citizens, do not exercise the privileges of citizenship. You see, not knowing some of the "secret" benefits, I probably would never have enjoyed the privileges of a guest in that beautiful Latin American hotel. The cost was too high. At least it *seemed* high to me before I discovered the secrets of that fabulous place. Thus, to one only superficially inititated into the kingdom or to one not a citizen of the kingdom at all, the *cost of the privileges* I have just listed is *much too high!* Even the most cursory examination of the kingdom of Jesus Christ reveals that the privileges are enjoyed in large measure as we experience the "costs" of citizenship.

8 The Price of the Privileges

The rich young ruler "went away sorrowing" when he discovered that for him the cost of the kingdom was the sale of his earthly goods. Because he did not understand the *innermost* secrets of the kingdom, he felt the price was *too high*. He did not buy. Any novice in the kingdom could have told him that the sale of his earthly goods would be compensated by access to the royal treasury of the universe. Everything that he would "give up" for the kingdom would be restored *one hundred times* plus have added to it the bonus of *eternal life* (Matthew 19:29). That poor young ruler! He missed the greatest investment of his life because he did not trust the King nor understand the secrets of kingdom economics.

Not *one* of the privileges described in the last chapter comes without a cost. And, I might add, the cost of each appears on the surface to be *outrageously expensive* if you don't understand kingdom economics. Let's examine a few price tags on kingdom privleges.

The Cost of Christ's Continuing Presence

Someone said recently, "If you are not so close to Christ as you used to be, you had better check to see who moved." The point is obvious. He is the anchor and we are the ships. One Bible teacher equates prayer with our drawing closer to Christ. He asked, "If we throw a boathook to the shore in order to close the distance, would anyone be so foolish as to propose that we are pulling the shore to the boat?"

Christ is *always* present with those who are citizens of the kingdom, but the *experiential reality* of that presence costs us dearly. The shore is always in the same place. But nearness to the shore in a sea whose currents are constantly pulling us from it depends on the exercise of our wills and meeting the cost of that presence.

The cost of that presence is *separation of ourselves from the attractions and lures of the world system, a life of holiness.* A life of holiness means, by very definition, a life of separation from evil, a life of separation from the entanglements of the kingdom of darkness. "Come out from among them and be ye separate," proclaims 2 Corinthians 6:17 (KJV), "and touch not the unclean thing." "Don't love the world system," cries the Apostle John, "or the love of the Father is not in you!" "Be holy because he is holy" commands Peter. The biblical authors are in agreement on this point. The price of experiencing the continuing and deepening presence of Christ is increasing distance from the evils of the world system. A tremendous price for many.

Demas forsook the cause of Christ because, "he loved this world" (2 Timothy 4:10). The good seed often fails to produce because the "cares of the this life and the deceitfulness of wealth" (Matthew 13:22) choke it. Just recently I heard of a young man who is leaving a Christian ministry because he "doesn't think one should have to live on a Christian worker's salary," and he wants to make money. Mark one giant step *away* from the experiencial presence of Christ.

I have known believers who wondered why they did not sense the reality of the presence of Christ in their lives as they clung tenaciously to their favorite secret sin, their favorite illicit relationship, their preoccupation with amassing an earthly fortune, their old friends, their position of status, their enslaving habits, their worldly "sophistication" or their favorite amusement and entertainment forms.

The price of the deepening presence of Christ for the Christian is the personal separation from any vestige of the world system that competes successfully with a total commitment to Christ.

The Cost of Exercising Divine Authority

One of the most exhilarating experiences for the Christian is to use divine authority to accomplish what God desires to have accomplished on the earth. "Resist the devil and he will run from you" declares James 4:7, but that promise presupposes that the Christian is in a position to exercise spiritual authority. I personally have seen my exercise of God's authority put the forces of evil—yes, even the occult powers—to flight. I have seen the exercise of spiritual authority silence a violent enemy of Christ, soften a hardened sinner, and effect a great victory for the cause of the kingdom. But these things happen only when one has paid the price of the exercise of God's authority. That price is *total abandonment of rebellion* and *complete submission* to the person and authority of Christ.

Satan laughs when a citizen of the kingdom presumes to exercise spiritual authority, the authority of Christ, from a state of mind and heart that is not totally in submission itself! It is only in the presence of the total dethronement of self that the enthronement of Christ and the consequent exercise of his power is accomplished. I have watched the powerful ministries of God's servants turn to tapioca pudding as they have become proud and impressed with their own abilities. Failure to submit *totally* to the authority of Christ over *every* area of life renders the citizen of the kingdom impotent and ineligible to proclaim authoritatively "Thus saith the Lord." Even a "silly millimeter" of rebellion or lack of submission turns that same "Thus saith the Lord" into an imperceptible squeak that threatens nei-

ther man nor beast. Many of those who stand in the pulpits
of North America are having virtually no eternal impact on
the lives and destinies of their parishioners. They are emit-
ting these imperceptible squeaks. When a servant of the
King, be he clergy or laity, surrenders to the sovereignty of
the Monarch and ceases from *all* rebellion, his softest whisper becomes a thundering roar. He speaks with the authority of the universe! But the price is great—surrender!

The Cost of Royal Family Relationships

When Jesus wanted to speak about the cost of discipleship
he almost always dealt with the cost in terms of human
relationships. In Luke 14:25-27, Jesus declared that unless a
person *hate* his father, mother, wife and children he could
not be a true disciple of his! This "hatred" is clarified to be
relative hatred in his teaching in Matthew 10:37,38. There he
states that the follower of Jesus must "love him more" than
father, mother, son or daughter. Jesus never advocated evil
motivation or hatred. He merely intended to dramatize the
point that the cost of enjoying the relationships of the royal
family is the *sacrificing of all competitive human relationships*.

Outrageous? Hardly. The sacrificing of the primacy of
human relationships to the divine ones, the surrender of
earthly relationships for heavenly ones, results in magnifi-
cent gain. I am an only child, so I never knew the rewarding
relationships between brother and sister. But, having become a citizen of the kingdom, I have entered into many
spiritual relationships with Christian brothers and sisters
all over the globe. Many of these are deeper than most of
the human brother-brother and brother-sister relationships
I have observed!

I personally think that Joseph of Arimathea was one
who discovered the cost and the rewards of kingdom relationships. No doubt someone in Joseph's family failed to

see the wisdom in Joseph's providing a newly-carved family tomb for this Jesus. "Now what have you done?" they may have asked. "Where are we going to bury grandfather now that you have given away the family tomb?" But Joseph, a "secret" believer in Jesus because of his fear of the Jews, knew that it was time to come forward and risk family disapproval. Identifying with Jesus had become more important to him than earthly relationships.

Job had to choose between a continuing good relationship with his wife and his obedience to the King and the royal family. Job's wife counseled, "Why don't you give up this religious fanaticism? Look where it is getting us. I recommend that you just curse God and die." Job had to choose whether he would pursue the earthly relationship or the heavenly one. He chose the latter and generations of the royal family have benefited from the decision! How many millions of citizens of the kingdom have been emboldened to carry on in the midst of suffering by Job's word, "Though he slay me yet will I trust in him"? Job's resolve had already cost him earthly, family relationships. But he knew that there was no net cost to such losses when the dividends were computed in!

The Cost of the Heavenly Inheritance

Amazing, wasn't it, how many wills showed up as embodiments of the disposition of the fortune of American billionaire Howard Hughes? At one point I heard that scores of documents had already surfaced. That number may be hundreds by now. People trying, through their own machinations, to get themselves "written in" to the wealth of Howard Hughes. So it is with the will of the universe, the inheritance of King Jesus. Millions of people are trying to benefit from that "co-inheritance" with Christ without ever paying the price of inheritance. Jesus tells us that the price of his kingdom is the *disclaiming of all earthly inheritance.*

Moses got into Hebrews 11, the great faith chapter, because he made a wise decision with regard to inheritance. He was, after all, raised in the palace and adopted by the daughter of the pharaoh. That would be good for a sizable share of the pharaoh's inheritance. But, we are told, Moses "regarded disgrace for the sake of Christ as of greater value than the treasures of Egypt, because he was looking ahead to his reward (Hebrews 11:26 NIV)." Did you get that? The basis on which he made the decision to turn his back on his earthly inheritance was that he was "looking ahead" to his reward. He understood kingdom economics. He knew that sacrificing an inheritance in one of the richest kingdoms in the history of the world was a wise decision. He knew that the inheritance he would receive from the King of kings would be greater than that of any pharaoh! Many, however, are not willing or able to turn their backs on the earthly inheritance.

Some people even try to gain both inheritances! They create "bogus wills" to the kingdom wealth. Jesus speaks of those in Matthew 7:21. "Not everyone who says, 'Lord, Lord' will enter the kingdom of heaven, but only he who does the will of my Father who is in heaven" (NIV). He adds that many will say to him on "that day" that they deserve to be included because the following validate their claims.

1. exercise of spiritual gifts *in his Name*;
2. exorcism of evil spirits;
3. performance of miracles.

Jesus plans to tell them plainly that he "never knew them" and that they should get away because they are "evildoers." The point is clear. Spiritual pizazz does not constitute kingdom citizenship. Only rebirth into the kingdom and the consequent renouncing of the earthly inheritance is sufficient basis on which to claim the heavenly inheritance. You can't have the best of both worlds, serve two masters, ride the fence, or collect the goodies from two wills. You choose. To some that choice bears too high a price tag. It is the price of all earthly ambition (Matthew 20:20-28).

The Cost of Drawing on the Royal Treasury

A contractor friend of mine told me the story of his early life as a poor newsboy in an Italian ghetto in the Northeast. At Christmas his teacher announced that they were going to be giving a Christmas food basket to a poor family and asked each child to bring something for the basket. My friend took nearly a whole week's profit from his newsroute and contributed a large can of peaches. His parents, poor and facing the toughest of times, scolded him for being so extravagant with the hard earned money the family needed. They were silenced on Christmas Eve when the food basket was delivered to their family!

I have thought oftentimes of the principle that story illustrates. It is a principle of kingdom economics. The cost of drawing on the royal treasury is *giving everything away from your own treasury*. For many that cost is too high.

The first year we were married, my wife and I tithed the income we received and experienced God's material blessing on the expensive first year of establishing a home. After calculating this blessing of God I said, "Honey, it isn't fair that God took care of us so well this year and we gave him only ten percent in return. What do you say we give him twenty percent this coming year?" She agreed and we embarked on a year of similar blessing despite the fact that we both were pursuing some schooling and had the usual expenses of homemaking. Near the end of that year I discovered that we had miscalculated and, with no more income coming in, we still owed God three hundred dollars. We apologized to God, told him that if he provided the money, we would give it all to him, and trusted. That Christmas a generous cash gift enabled us to pay God the three hundred dollars plus his twenty percent of the overage!

Then I embarked on a test of kingdom economics. I had read from the teachings of Jesus that the amount disbursed from the kingdom treasury was in direct proportion to the amount disbursed from my personal treasury in acts of worship to the King. Was not that the point of the "good measure principle" established in Luke 6:38? Jesus said, "Give, and it will be given to you. A good measure, pressed down, shaken together, and running over, will be poured into your lap. For with the measure you use, it will be measured to you" (NIV). I reasoned that if we gave in ten or twenty percent portions, we could expect to receive in ten or twenty percent portions. If we gave more, we could receive more from the royal treasury. We could choose to give with a teaspoon or a semi-truck. We would receive back either a heaping teaspoon or a heaping semi-truckload. We could determine that.

My wife and I started increasing the percentage given each year by five percent "so long as God enabled us." I won't tell you how incredibly high that percentage became before God finally changed the whole basis of our ecomonics (because he knew he had everything). But when we passed the fifty percent level, we had a tax problem because we had to pay Uncle Sam tax on money we were giving away. When I went to a tax attorney friend of mine for counsel, he could not believe we were giving as much as I said we were. He knew how well we were living and generally what my income was. He knew it was impossible. And it was.

Living by kingdom economics is always impossible. When you learn the secrets of the kingdom, they defy all reason and all the principles of the earthly kingdom. God met my family's need time after time after time when we gave our "last dollar" to him. I was given a new Oldsmobile. God increased the value of the house we bought nearly one hundred percent in five years to quadruple our equity. He chose a mansion of a new house for us at $11,000 under the bank's appraised value. He also cut down our expenses by keeping our six-person family free of sickness for years. And all this was done while my annual income remained the same or even dropped!

One caution: the repayment is not always in the same medium of exchange as the investment. If it were, we would be tempted to use God as a "get rich quick" device. God's response to material investment may well be non-material blessing. If so, it's of even greater value. Who would trade, say, a few thousand dollars for good health, family peace or spiritual power?

Jesus declared in Matthew 19:23-26 that it is impossible for rich people to enter the kingdom of heaven. He knew that for a person with many earthly goods the price of gaining access to the royal treasury is too high. It is signing over the ownership of the entire earthly fortune to the King. The only hope for the rich person is a supernatural work in his life. It was in *this* context that Jesus said, "With God all things are possible."

The parables of the treasure in the field and the pearl of infinite price recorded in Matthew 13:44-46 explain how this supernatural impossibility takes place. These are kingdom parables. Jesus was teaching that when a person discovers the kingdom, it is like discovering a great treasure in a field. In modern parlance that is like discovering oil on a piece of land. It is like a pearl merchant discovering a pearl so incredibly beautiful and large that it is priceless. In both parables the finders "sold everything they had" to own the treasure. So the price of kingdom citizenship and access to the royal treasure is everything you have for everything you want.

The Cost of Exercising the Priestly Office

The glorious privilege of "bridging the spiritual gap" between the unbeliever and the one High Priest is not without cost. Just as there are qualifications for every priesthood, so there are qualifications for this priestly office. But for some the cost seems extravagantly high. It must seem that way or more citizens of the kingdom would be exercising the privilege.

Did you ever stop to do some basic mathematics on this point? If you were to take the average body of believers of, say, one hundred people and calculate the extent to which they are introducing others to kingdom citizenship, you should see some dramatic numbers appear. For instance, if each of the one hundred person assembly introduced just one person to Christ that affiliated with the assembly each three months, the body of believers would be quadrupling every year! If this ratio could be maintained on an almost continuous geometric progression the ranks of that church would outswell the Houston Astrodome in a few short years.

When we realize that the typical church stays pretty much the same for decades, we do not have to be too intelligent to figure out that somebody—a whole lot of somebodies—are not exercising the priestly office of kingdom citizenship! Unless they feel the cost is too high, why wouldn't they be engaging in bringing others to the King and seeing them reborn into the kingdom! The cost is too high for most Christians. The cost of exercising the priestly office is *total abandonment of all self-righteousness and alien religious notions.*

The reason I know that the price is too high for the typical Christian is that I was one of those "cheap" kingdom citizens for eighteen years. As I mentioned earlier, in that period of time I did not see more than five people enter the kingdom through my exercise of the priestly office. The reason I did not was that I did not want to give up all of my self-righteousness and biblical knowledge. After all, I was Bible taught, seminary trained, doctrinally pure and proud of it. I used to win theological arguments with "the Old Testament tied behind my back" only to watch those vanquished victims walk away from the kingdom. I could not understand it. I used to lick my chops when some cynic would bait me with, "You do not really believe the Bible is infallible, do you?" or "You mean you think Jonah really was swallowed by a big fish and burped up three days later alive?" But my best cases in defense of God and his thinking seemed to fall on deaf ears. Why not? To those unbelievers this was just another religious argument. The human priest was the visible one; the Great High Priest, the Priest-King and his Spirit were obscured.

Today I have to bite my lip to avoid using ten years of post-high-school education in dealing with unbelievers about entrance into the kingdom! I am now using simple verses from the Bible like John 3:16 because I have discovered that exercising the priestly office comes only at the expense of my own self-righteousness and intellectual pride. If I make a "religious" challenge, I get a "religious" response. If I make an intellectual challenge, I get an intellectual response. If I present the simple gospel of the Kingdom in the power of the Holy Spirit, I get a kingdom response wrought by the Holy Spirit. A citizen is added to the kingdom. Jesus declared in Matthew 5:20 that no self-righteous person would get into the kingdom. Surely no self-righteous person will exercise the priestly office of a kingdom citizen.

No citizen of the kingdom will exercise the office of priest if he is all tied up in rule-keeping either. That was another one of my problems. I was so proud of the things I did and did not do and so "superior" to those whose rule keeping differed from mine, that I was an offense to the kingdom. Paul tried desperately to get this concept through the heads of the Galatians and Romans. In Romans 14:17-18 he declared:

> For the kingdom of God is not a matter of eating or drinking, but of righteousness, peace and joy in the Holy Spirit, because anyone who serves Christ in this way is pleasing to God and approved by men (NIV).

It is the rules that we keep and the attendant righteousness we ascribe to keeping them that form the core of false "religion" which must go in order for us to be functioning as a nation of priests. High price.

The Cost of Access to God's Secrets

On an airplane flight some time ago I was seated next to a very intellectual man. He was the head of one of the nation's great nuclear laboratories and was a world honored nuclear physicist. As we got acquainted, I began to share my faith in Christ with him. He was polite and gave me a "that is an interesting theory" kind of response. So I backed off and we talked amicably about other topics until the meal service silenced our conversation. In the midst of the meal he turned to me and said, "I do not know how people can be so blasé! Do you realize the physical forces that are in play at this moment right here? Why this enormous aircraft is sailing 35,000 feet above the earth held aloft by physical principles of aviation. This cabin is controlled to a comfortable temperature, the atmosphere controlled to a perfect pressure, and the meal cooked in such a way that the cold food is cold and the hot food is hot. How can the people on a plane like this be so oblivious to all this?"

"I was thinking something similar," I replied. "As I was eating, I was looking out there at those beautiful, snow capped mountains and wondering how you could be so oblivious to the fact that I have a personal relationship with the One that spoke those mountians into existence!" He looked at me as if he had just been punched. After processing what I had said for a few moments through that genius mind of his, he replied, "*That* is the same message that my black cleaning lady gives me."

How wonderful. I was communicating with this intellectual, Ph.D. to Ph.D., but when it came to the Gospel of the kingdom, the secrets I had learned I shared with his presumably uneducated black cleaning lady. Hallelujah! God chose the simple things of the world to confound the wise. He granted the deep secrets of the universe to the citizens of his kingdom to the extent that they would abandon their earthly wisdom. That is the price of access to God's secrets, *total abandonment of the world's wisdom*.

No citizen of the kingdom is ever liberated by the innermost secrets of the King so long as he scrutinizes them, criticizes them, compromises them or seeks to "fit them into contemporary scientific thought." Scientific thought must be fitted into the secrets of the King or it will continue to be scientific nonsense. The Apostle Paul paid the price and reaped the rewards. He declared to his Corinthian brethren:

> When I came to you, brothers, I did not come with
> eloquence or superior wisdom as I proclaimed to you
> the testimony of God . . . my message and my preach-

ing were not with wise and persuasive words, but with a demonstration of the Spirit's power, so that your faith might not rest on men's wisdom but on God's power (Corinthians 2:1-5 NIV).

For the learned and intellectually proud, the price is *too high*.

What do you think? Is kingdom citizenship something to be desired? Is the cost of kingdom privileges worth the rewards of their exercise? From the vantage point of twenty-nine years as a citizen of the kingdom and nearly six years of testing these kingdom principles, I declare for all the world to hear, *Yes, Yes, A Thousand Times Yes!* Pay it!

Having paid it, examine how this will liberate you from the "double jeopardy" of serving simultaneously under the constraints of the kingdom of heaven and the strictures of a human government. Can you imagine a person:

1. spiritually detached from the evils of the world system and experiencing the reality of the presence of Christ;
2. free from all spirit of rebellion and joyfully submissive to the authority of Christ in his life;
3. liberated from the "constraints" of earthly relationships only to bathe those relationships in kingdom love;
4. totally released from any expectation of earthly inheritance and living in hope for the heavenly one;
5. giving away all he possesses in the glorious release provided by underwriting from the kingdom treasury;
6. free from all self-righteousness and phony rule-keeping to share the Good News with everyone who will listen; and
7. released from the restraints of the academic "party

line" to share freely the kingdom secrets with all who seek wisdom?

Will *this* person be a troublemaker for a human government? Only if that government chooses to make him so. His kingdom citizenship will make him an asset to any earthly kingdom; his righteousness will exalt that nation!

9 The Future Tense of the Present Tenseness

Some years ago I heard a talk entitled, "The practical value of predictive prophecy." The speaker told how much we rely on accurate predictions of future happenings in the stock markets, weather forecasts and insurance actuarial tables. He contrasted this with the relatively little attention given to the prophetic Scriptures which, by the way, comprise forty percent of the Bible. It is the continuous flow of history written "before it happens" that gives the Scriptures the "feel of the ages." Without this context we have little understanding of God's eternal plan. We are caught in a fragmentary view of life "as it affects me today" rather than life as it affects eternity.

One observer of contemporary believers says that we are a "cut flower generation." This is a generation that possesses the beauty of true believers but has been cut off from the historical and foundational roots which created its beauty. As such, the generation is destined to be unproductive and shortly unattractive. The King never intended for it to be that way! The King intended that the message of the kingdom be a longitudinal view—a panorama rather than a peek, a movie rather than a snapshot—of his plans. I do not think it is even possible to understand what is happening in the world today unless one understands the past, present and future tenses of the kingdom plan.

John Bright, in his book, *The Kingdom of God,* states

that "the concept of the kingdom of God involves, in a real sense, the total message of the Bible" and that "Old Testament and New Testament thus stand together as the two acts of a single drama. Had we to give that book a title, we might with justice call it, 'The Book of the Coming Kingdom of God,' That is indeed, the central theme everywhere."

It surely would be strange for any book to start, "In the beginning . . ." and to end "Even so, come, Lord Jesus." if the authors did not intend to give the readers a sense of time perspective! Without this perspective, life is like stepping into a movie without knowing when it began, when it will end or how the events that are unfolding fit into the plot. Might as well forget the story and just enjoy the popcorn!

Our Master apparently did not feel that "just enjoying the popcorn" was a sufficient motivation for participating in the unfolding drama of the ages. He obviously wanted us to know what was going on in the plot. So the Book is sprinkled with narratives of his past, present and future dealings with the race. The pages are covered with time and event references such as "in the last days," "when the fullness of time was come," "heaven and earth shall pass away," "from before the foundations of the world," and "before Abraham was I am."

In the midst of this time-event consciousness is the six o'clock news. It is news of increasing turmoil in the Middle East, increasing military grass fires around the globe, and nations and races rising up against nations and races. To presume for a minute that the "current events" have no roots in the eternal plan of God for the world would be a slap in the face to an eternal God. The front page of the paper is rooted in the kingdom and the plan which began before the world was. The "international report" on TV reflects the moving of the hand of God in nations as much as the fiery pillar and cloud indicated the moving of God to the wilderness Israelites. The increasing pressure of international diplomacy reflects the convergence of universal forces toward a climax as much as the convergence of physical forces indicated the impending creation in Genesis 1.

The "Present Tenseness" of the Kingdom

But the present tenseness is not just in the world system. There is an increasing tenseness in the church of Jesus Christ worldwide. Certain trends are so obvious that few leaders in the cause of Christ fail to observe them. I do not know a single Christian leader who does not observe that there is a greater harvest going on in the world today than at any time in the history of the Church.

In countries where missionaries once burned themselves out for lifetimes to see a handful of results, there is now a spiritual harvest that seems to know few bounds. I just heard of a man who is trusting God to raise up 10,000 missionaries from Nagaland (find that on your map!) to reach out from that near territory of India to the unreached masses of Asia. God is putting the awakenings in Indonesia, Colombia, South Korea, New Guinea, Uganda and sub-Saharan Africa on the spiritual "six o'clock news" for all the world to see.

At the same time the increasing pressure of militant atheism is "tightening the screws" on the open Christian witness. There is more persecution of Christians in more countries than at any time in church history. And this is happening as the citizens of the kingdom come closer to fulfilling the Great Commission than ever before.

A friend of mine is dreaming of the day when every creature will hear of the saving grace of Jesus Christ and is working toward that end. He is a man who has made a good living exploiting the potential of satellite technology to serve the agricutural needs of the world. He shared the tenseness of things in the kingdom in a graph which described the increasing communication potential of the world. It was a bar graph which indicated that the anticipated electronic media market via satellite for the 1980 Moscow Olympics was 3.9 billion people! That means that communicating with the world's 4.2 billion people is now a very clear possibility. But on the graph past 1980 was a large question mark and the words "war in space?" The advent of "killer satellites" that can destroy the communication, surveillance and security satellites of other countries is also here. Whether this amazing satellite communication potential can be used for the Great Commission before the "war in space" destroys the potential is a matter of speculation. The tenseness continues.

I took my family to a musical production some time ago and I was stirred by the similarity of that event to the present situation in the kingdom. The audience buzzed loudly in the fully-lit theatre as the "last minute" people hastened to their seats. The house lights flickered as a signal to the audience and then began to dim. The "chit chat" waned as the footlights flooded the closed curtain. In the orchestra pit a strange cacophony of sounds indicated that each member of the orchestra was making sure that his instrument was in tune for the first number of the musical. You could sense the electricity in the air as the orchestra pit fell silent, joining the silence of the audience seated in the blackened theatre. The curtain was about to open, but nobody knew exactly when.

The world is growing dark. The flicker of world events is signaling to a global audience that the spectacle of the ages is about to begin. Every advance notice and the clear indications of the Program suggest that this will be a tragedy *and* a comedy, bringing tears to some and exhilaration to others. In the orchestra pit the members of Christ's "musicians' union" are creating considerable noise (but not much harmony). Each member seeks to get his instrument in tune, adjusting it in his own style. Any minute now the Director will give the cue and the curtain will part. But nobody knows when. What *is* known is that it will open. All of the elaborate preparations, all of these gathered people, all of those distributed announcements and all of those endless rehearsals did not occur just to provide this moment of electric expectation. Any minute now it is *going* to happen. There is a future tense to all this.

The Future Tense

The curtain is going to open. So there is a future tense to the present situation in the Body of Christ. So what? How can we know what to expect? Perhaps it would be good to summarize some of the uncompleted events on the program of the kingdom, just to help us keep perspective.

First of all, the Great Commission is to be fulfilled. It has not happened yet, but Jesus made it clear that it has to happen. He said that there were three prophecies that had to be fulfilled (Luke 24:45-47). They were the suffering of the Messiah, his resurrection from the dead on the third day, *and* the proclamation of "repentance and forgiveness for sins" in all nations beginning at Jerusalem. The first two prophecies are now history. At this writing the third is still future.

In Matthew 24:14 Jesus indicated that the "gospel of the kingdom shall be preached in all the world for a witness to all nations and *then* shall the end come [emphasis added]." While the sequence of events is unclear at a number of points, the reality of the fulfillment of the Great Commission is not. Nor is it unclear that its fulfillment is in the top part of the list of future events!

Second, we know that the King's return is still future. There is more prophetic support for the second coming of Christ than there was for his first coming. Christ's own integrity is at stake on this issue. He made certain that we understood that if he went away, he would "surely come again" and receive us unto himself (John 14:3). The two men who appeared at Christ's ascension assured the onlookers that "this same Jesus" (not some substitute or imposter) would come in the same manner as he left!

Third, the Guidebook is clear that there will be an end to things as we know them in this "present age." Scores of prophetic events could be subsumed under this category: everything from the passing away of the earth to the rise of the Man of Sin, from the judgment of the nations to the resurrection of the saints. Let it suffice to say that there is going to be a dramatic and catastrophic change in the entire world system and in the order of the universe as it relates to the world and its inhabitants.

Fourth, the King will establish a literal reign over the universe that will not end even in eternity. This kingdom will have different operational dimensions throughout the sequence of prophetic events. They will never again be "shared or "delegated" in the same sense that the Prince of this World now realizes certain dominion over part of the King's territory. Every knee will bow and every tongue will confess that Jesus is total sovereign of the world and universe (Philippians 2:9-11). There will be a finality about this that will be unshakable.

The Marriage

The present situation in the kindgom is like the situation in a far-off land where a romantic drama is taking place. Some years ago the parents of a lovely young girl made arrangements with a royal family from another country for the marriage of their children. The young girl, a commoner, was to marry the son of the noble family, a prince. The marriage was arranged while the children were still small, as is the custom in that part of the world.

The young man and woman met in childhood, but it was a fickle friendship that ended in no particular lasting relationship. However, it was clear that the prince was increasingly committed to the young girl. Years later the two met in adulthood and the prince took the romantic initiative. He offered the young lady his kingdom and his life as an evidence of his love. The young lady, still not ready to respond immediately to the offer of marriage, did accept the prince's proposal. She permitted a betrothal and promised to marry the prince the next time he returned.

The prince left the young lady, whom he dearly loved, to pursue his father's business. One day he would receive his father's kingdom and would be able to return to claim his bride. He promised a great, royal celebration at their wedding and left his foremost assistant with the lady to comfort her, protect her and prepare her for the great marriage to be consumated upon his return.

From time to time the land has buzzed with rumors of the return of the prince-to-be-king. Each time the evidences of the prince's return reach the land, the heart of the lady stirs within her. Will this be the year? Will the prince return now? Has he received the crown from his father as he said?

Each time the rumors pass, other questions enter the lady's mind. Can she trust the prince? Will he really return for her? What if things don't work out as the prince said they would? Despite all these questions and rumors the prince's assistant assures the lady that the prince is trust-worthy, that he *will* return. The marriage will be consummated and the wedding celebration will be even greater than she can imagine.

This is where we find the Church of Jesus Christ. Before the foundations of the world, the marriage between Christ and his Church was arranged. Though Christ and his bride-to-be had met many times before, no lasting relationship resulted until in "adulthood" Christ offered his life and kingdom to his beloved. His beloved, rejecting the idea of an immediate ceremony, agreed to a betrothal which would terminate in marriage when Christ would return as King. In the interim, Christ has left his Holy Spirit to comfort, protect and prepare the Church for the marriage.

We are in a state of suspense. After many rumors of our lover's return in the past, it is now clear that he cannot delay much longer. His Assistant assures us this is true. Will this kingdom come to us this year?

10 The Plot Sickens

Enter: The Villain. Into that beautiful little story of the prince and the lady must come, I am sorry to say, another character. He is a jealous, proud, evil suitor from the land of the prince. Years ago he had a "falling out" with the prince's father, the king. He was caught in an attempt to overthrow the king and establish himself on the throne. Exiled by the king from his homeland, he came to live and rule in the land of the lady. He has ruled for many years in a cruel, vengeful and capricious way.

Bad though it is that the villain should rule evilly, he also seeks to do evil to the prince, to the lady and to their intended plans for marriage. Through lies, deceit and trickery he has sought to violate the chastity of the lady and keep the prince from becoming king. He badgers the subjects of the realm and diverts their minds from the prince's return and the anticipated wedding ceremony.

The villain's endeavors have not been without success. Were it not for the efforts of the prince's faithful assistant to alert the bride-to-be, things would be far worse than they are. As it is, there are a host of enemies, both inside and outside the lady's family, that are hindering the plans for the marriage.

A look around the realm uncovers a motley assortment of enemies of the marriage with an equally motley assortment of motives. Some even profess to be friends of the prince and the lady, but still impede preparations for the wedding! Our survey reveals . . .

The Doctrinalites

They profess to be the truest friends of the prince. The Doctrinalites are so totally preoccupied with analyzing, organizing, exegeting and debating the content of the prince's love letters that they are not contributing one whit to the preparations for the marriage. I can hear them now arguing vehemently over whether the prince is indicating in his third love letter that he might return *before* or *after* the next leap year. It really shouldn't matter to them. They won't be ready anyway, unless they set aside the acrimony and get involved in the ceremony.

The Denominationalites

Within the lady's own family are the Denominationalites. They have divided the family and prospective guests into factions over whose relatives will sit where at the wedding feast. Some of the factions are not even speaking to each other because they are splits off those who are splits off those who are splits off . . . . Couldn't they just now, as the prince's return seems so imminent, put off the feuds and "pitch in" a bit and help with the preparations? "No such luck," we say, when one of the Denominationalites corrects us with the proud declaration that his denomination doesn't believe in luck. It feels the concept undercuts the sovereignty of God. Oh well, let's look elsewhere for those who are helping with the preparations.

The Nationalites

The Nationalites are to be found both inside and outside the lady's family. They are infected with a strange kind of virus that creates delusions of national supremacy. Some are refusing to cooperate in the preparations for the return of the prince with those from other parts of the realm or from other provinces. Some overzealous Nationalites are trampling over the territories of others. They profess to be proclaiming the good news of the impending wedding but are mixing the message with their own national flag waving. Others, the more passive types, have called a "moratorium" on *all* messengers from outside their own realm. They insist that the only people suitable to proclaim messages are those from their own nation.

The Intellectualites

There is not much help for the marriage preparations coming from the Intellectualites. They have been spending years now theorizing and researching to prove academically that the alleged relationship between the prince and the lady is totally mythical. They also conjecture that the prince, if alive at all, has no plans to return except in the minds and memories of the populace. They claim to have "demythologized" the prince's love letters to discover that there is no sound, intellectual basis for belief in the return.

The Racites

The first four groups we have identified have been preoccupied with notions that have kept them from participation in the marriage preparations. The next groups we found will really stun you. They are not just *passively distracted* from the wedding preparations, they are *aggressively opposed* to them! The Racites are in this group of the active opposition.

You see, the Racites feel that fellowship and cooperation must follow racial lines. They oppose the marriage because of the "inferior lineage" of (a) the prince—anti-Semitism is not uncommon in their ranks, (b) the lady—

the lady's family is a mix of noble and ignoble racial strains, and (c) the messengers that brought them the good news of the wedding plans. It is not uncommon among those Racites who want to believe the beautiful story of the prince and the lady to proclaim that "discoveries prove" the prince is of their (pure) race.

The Technocrites

The Technocrites have always been opposed to the story of the prince and the lady. They have felt all along that such romantic ideals have no place in a "scientific and technological society." They mouth contemptuous remarks about the story not bearing up under the tests of the "scientific method" or not fitting into their "empirical observations." They proclaim that the "new wave of technology" will usher in a standard of living every bit as good as that of any prince from a far-off land. "Trust science," they say.

The Democratites

Another strange breed of people in the realm are the Democratites. They so mix their beliefs about the prince and the lady with their own political ideals that they have become enemies of the marriage. They oppose it on the basis that the prince is from a non-democratic society (a kingdom) and that he is soon to be, if not already, a dictator (king). They have even insisted unrealistically that those countries that receive the news of the marriage should respond by adopting democratic political systems.

The Socialites

Not unlike the Democratites in some ways, the Socialites also mix their political ideals with their views of the marriage and of the prince. They believe in the exaltation of "the state." The state should be supreme in any political arrangement. Consequently, they oppose the marriage because the wedding plan was not originated by and is not to be held under the auspices of the state.

The Marxite-Leninites

One radical offshoot of the Socialites is the Marxite-Leninites. The "MLs" vehemently oppose the marriage because they're convinced that (a) the prince and his father (the king) do not exist, (b) princes are part of the bourgeoisie, and (c) the romantic story and wedding preparations are keeping the people from building a better *material order* in society. Why trust in "pie in the sky by and by" when you can carve out your own kingdom through materialistic self-effort? "Trust in the state and in the Marxite-Leninite doctrines," they say.

The Liberationites

An even more radical group opposed to the marriage and wedding preparations are the Liberationites. Their opposition is rooted in a basic rejection of all traditional or "establishment" values. If it is established, it is the enemy. For people to be truly "free," they must be "liberated from the shackles of traditional thinking." The present institutional forms of government, economics, religion, morality and social structure are a hindrance to individual freedom. Liberationites oppose the marriage because it is rooted in traditional values such as love, marriage, family, the divine right of kings and the existence of realms beyond their own. They feel obligated to liberate others from belief in the "prince-marriage myth."

The Revolutionites

Near relatives of the Liberationites are the Revolutionites. They oppose the marriage because plans for it are "dulling the revolutionary fervor of the people." There is no time for love stories when there are governments to be over-thrown and violence to be created.

Well, there you have it: the grim spectacle of many groups that are opposed to the marriage for a variety of motivations. It is obvious that the villain has had his part in the formulation and propagation of many of the notions espoused by these groups. Sometimes one would get the impression that there was no one left in the realm that trusted the prince, the lady or the marriage story. That is not the case. There are many who are deeply committed to the prince, the lady and the marriage preparations. They are actively working to spread the good news of the wedding and to convince the sceptics and scoffers of the reality of it all. These are the Disciplites.

The Disciplites

There is a faithful group of people who simply and loyally are commited to the prince and the lady. They distinguish themselves immediately from the opposing groups by the following attributes:

1. *They all have met the prince personally.* They, there-fore, are not working on "hearsay evidence." They know the prince and have been touched by his obvious virtue. They have been recipients of his kindness and continually talk of the favor that he extended to them even though they were originally his enemies.

2. *They stick close to the prince's assistant.* They hang on every word of the assistant. They submit themselves to his positive influence in their lives and follow his instruction and directions as best they can. "After all," they proclaim, "in the absence of the prince we certainly should rely on the direction of the prince's chosen representative!"

3. *They communicate frequently with the prince themselves.* Not willing to go on rumors and idle tales about the prince, his return, the marriage and the kingdom, they faithfully communicate with him. They pore over the letters they have received from him and ask his assistant to help them understand and implement the instructions of the prince for them.

4. *They live for the day of the marriage and the coming of the kingdom to them.* They know that their faithfulness to the prince will be handsomely rewarded. No kingdom in their own realm can compare with the kingdom that the prince will bring to them when he returns as king to marry the lady. They are indomitable and unquenchable in their hope while the other "ites" around them are defeated and despairing. They have a transcendent glow about them and a set of values that puts relationships above every other consideration in their lives. Some have noted that they are even taking on some of the personal characteristics of the prince! Imagine that!

And how do the Disciplites respond to the many opposing groups with their false notions of the prince and marriage? They humbly and lovingly, but with *real conviction*, proclaim the truth as they know it. It is not a matter of fighting error in fleshly self-effort. It is a matter of openly declaring the story. "Truth," someone has said, "is like a lion. It does not need to be defended. Merely let it loose and it will defend itself!"

11 The Power and the Glory

It's often called the "thrill of victory." It is a description of the joy of winning, which every human being finds to be a natural "high" to his human spirit. I've watched men and boys shout in victory over their bottle cap games in the slums of Asia. I've seen hundreds of thousands of fans go wild over the victory of their Olympic champion. I've sat in the Super Bowl and watched my team overwhelm the opposition and emerge victorious. I remember the sirens, shouts, horns and parades that signaled the end of World War II. Every athletic coach can tell you that despite those elusive and transcendent values to be gained from just "playing the game," the purpose of playing is *winning*.

It is my deep conviction that within the human spirit the Creator has implanted the need to win. I believe that God has created within us a "victory vacuum." This vacuum creates everything from poor self images to educational underachievers if it is not fed. "Nothing succeeds like success" is a statement of educational verity. So those who deal with the educationally deprived seek to create environments of *victory* in the learning context. It works because only personal *victory* fills the "victory vacuum."

I remember an experience I had while running high school cross-country. It was a beautiful two-mile run through the woods and over the meadows and hills to the finish line. There were always a large number of competitors at the starting line and always a straggling few at the finish.

I remember a race in which I was letting a competitor set the pace for the race because it was just slightly faster than my own. I stayed just a pace or two behind him for the entire course. When he speeded up, I speeded up. When he slowed down, I slowed down. The only time I passed him was up a sandy hill. I had learned that a "show of strength" on that hill was a powerful demoralizer. That hill on the second mile was the "end of the race" for the faint.

We were now heading into the last quarter mile, and from my vantage point just behind him, I could see his body weakening. His arms were beginning to droop and his breath was coming in long, desperate gasps, but he was maintaining the pace. To a spectator, it surely looked like he was winnning. I knew differently. I had been measuring my own pace and testing my own strength throughout the distance. One of my strengths as a runner was the ability to put on a sprint for the last nearly quarter of a mile and leave most others behind. I calculated the moment for the start of my sprint. Despite my weariness and weakness, I knew I had the sprint left. At the precise, premeditated moment, I broke for the tape, passing him in a couple of strides and hitting the tape still widening the distance between us. *Victory!* It was worth it, no matter how badly it hurt!

The kingdom is like that. The King is, from all secular observations, lagging behind in the race for the conquest of the world and the minds and spirits of men. The kingdom runners seem like a weary pack hanging just off the shoulder of the Enemy as we enter the last quarter mile to the tape. But we all must know that we are *winning!*

Our King created us for *victory*. Our King prophesied our *victory*. Our King taught us to expect *victory*. When it appeared as if our King had been defeated, he arose from the dead in *victory*. Our King is in heaven being acclaimed for his *victory*, and he is coming again in *victory*. He fully expects to "burst for the tape" at the precise, premeditated moment to overwhelm the forces of this world and attain *victory!*

Jesus taught *victory* in a number of ways. He said in Matthew 13 that the wheat would emerge victorious from among the weeds. The weeds would be gathered together and burned "at the end of this age." He said that the wheat was the "children of the kingdom" and that the weeds were the "children of the wicked one." His angels, he said, "would gather out of his kingdom everything that would offend."

In that same chapter Jesus taught that victory would come to those true believers caught in the kingdom dragnet (Mathew 13:47-51). The righteous would be gathered into vessels, but the wicked would be "cast away" into a "furnace of fire" with "wailing and gnashing of teeth."

In Luke 10, Jesus described the victory scene of the ages when he said, "I saw Satan fall from heaven like lightning. See, I give you authority to trample on snakes and scorpions and to overpower the enemy totally; nothing will harm you" (personal paraphrase of verses 18-19). He added to this a word in John 16:33, "In this world you will have trouble. But take heart! I have overcome the world" (NIV).

The Apostle Paul describes our victory as follows:

For as in Adam all die, so in Christ all will be made alive. But each in his own turn: Christ, the first fruits; then, when he comes, those who belong to him. Then the end will come, when he hands over the kingdom to God the Father after he has destroyed all dominion, authority and power. For he must reign until God has put all his enemies under his feet (1 Corinthians 15:22-25 NIV).

The Apostle John adds this note:

The kingdom of the world has become the kingdom of our Lord and of his Christ, and he will reign forever

and ever . . . . We give thanks to you . . . because you
have taken your great power and have begun to reign
(Revelation 11:15-17 NIV).

VICTORY!

The Greatness of Our Kingdom

Victory for what? Victory for victory's sake? Victory to enjoy some perverse jubilation at the expense of our foes?
Victory only to return to the quiet desperation of mundane
human existence? Hardly. Victory to establish the kingdom. Victory to enter it. Victory to enjoy it forever. Victory
to enjoy the KING forever.

Not many realize the greatness of the kingdom which
is soon to be ours. I didn't until in seminary I studied with
the author of a book titled, *The Greatness Of The Kingdom*.
Dr. Alva J. McClain in a chapter called, "The Blessings of
the Prophetic Kingdom" captures the fabulous features of
the kingdom better than any other author I have read. In
his lead paragraph to the chapter, Dr. McClain observes
that the establishment of the kingdom will:

> . . . bring about sweeping and radical changes in every
> department of human activity; so far reaching that
> Isaiah speaks of its arena as "a new earth" (Isaiah
> 65:17). Every need of humanity will be anticipated and
> provided for. "Before they call," God says, "I will
> answer" (Isaiah 65:24) . . . . no legitimate aspect of hu-
> man life will be left without the regal saving activity
> (Isaiah 33:6 ASV).

Universal Joy

God's outpouring of his grace on mankind through the
King will result in worldwide and universal joy. The King
will be comforting all those who mourn, and providing the

"oil of joy for mourning, the spirit of praise for the spirit of heaviness" (Isaiah 61:2,3). Jeremiah observed that the redeemed " . . . shall come and sing . . . their soul shall be as a watered garden; and they shall not sorrow any more at all" (Jeremiah 31:12).

Universal Social Justice

The King will make sure that there is a full and complete equalization of social benefits. The parasites and "robber barons" of our society will be done away, as Isaiah describes it, so that people " . . . shall build houses, and inhabit them; and they shall plant vineyards, and eat the fruit of them. They shall not build, and another inhabit; they shall not plant and another eat" (Isaiah 65:21,22).

Worldwide Reclamation of Ecology

Wherever man has stepped, he has trampled the earth with his destructive heel and has left his wasteful imprint on ecology. The King will take care of that in the kingdom. Isaiah describes how, "They shall build the old wastes, they shall raise up the former desolations, and they shall repair the waste cities, the desolations of many generations" (Isaiah 61:4). The slums and cancerous sores of the cities will be healed: "They of the city shall flourish like the grass of the earth" (Psalm 72:16).

International Governing Authority

Knowing that even in the best of moral and spiritual climates there is a need for coordination and direction (even in the Godhead this is true), the King has purposed to serve as his own United Nations. "And it shall come to pass in the latter days, . . . he will judge between the nations, and will decide concerning many peoples" (Isaiah 2:2,4 ASV).

Since all of the King's decisions will be perfect, there will be no need for human warfare. Military science as a study will be obsolete because "Neither shall they learn war any more" (Isaiah 2:4).

A Universal Language

Every hindrance to worldwide peace and communication will be removed and the frustrating barriers of language will be abolished. The prophet saw the coming of the kingdom as a time when God would " ... turn to the people a pure language that they may call upon the name of Jehovah, to serve him with one consent" (Zephaniah 3:9, ASV).

Worldwide Agricultural Productivity

The Old Testament prophets were clear in foreseeing abundant rainfall coming at regular and predictable seasons (Joel 2:21-24; Ezekiel 34:26). There will be ample streams of water in even the unlikely places of the earth such as on "every high hill and mountain" (Isaiah 30:25), in the desert, on the parched ground and in the thirsty land (Isaiah 35:6,7). Ezekiel saw a miraculous stream flowing out of the temple (Ezekiel 47:1-12), while Zechariah saw that stream flowing perennially toward the seas (Zechariah 14:8).

The ample provision of moisture in all seasons will no doubt be part of the explanation of the kingdom's abundant agricultural productivity. The desert "shall rejoice" and shall "blossom as a rose" (Isaiah 35:1,2 ASV). Even the most unproductive places of the earth shall flourish. The Psalmist describes corn and fruit "upon the top of the mountains" (Psalm 72:16), and Isaiah attributes the luxuriant productivity to the supernatural "pouring" of God's Spirit "from on high" making the "wilderness a fruitful field" (Isaiah 32:15).

Universal Elimination of Physical Disease and Deformity

The kingdom will solve all problems of physical deformity. "The eyes of the blind shall be opened, and the ears of the deaf shall be unstopped. Then shall the lame man leap as a hart, and the tongue of the dumb sing" (Isaiah 35:5,6). There will be no disease for "the inhabitant shall not say, 'I am sick'" (Isaiah 33:24).

Total Providential Control of Accidents

Even in a morally good society there is still the possibility of tragedy through ordinary living hazards and accidental causes. This is no problem in the kingdom! There will be nothing to fear from animals, for God will have them "dwell safely in the wilderness and sleep in the woods" (Ezekiel 34:2). The wild or "evil" beasts God will have caused to "cease from the land" (Ezekiel 34:25). The changes in the animal world will enable the wolf to "dwell with the lamb" and the leopard to "lie down with the kid." A "little child shall lead them and the suckling child shall play on the hole of the asp" (Isaiah 11:6,8)! Even the eating habits of dangerous beasts will be changed as "the lion shall eat straw like the ox" (Isaiah 11:7).

The promise of Psalm 91 shall be fulfilled that God will give his angels charge over kingdom citizens lest they "dash a foot against a stone" (Psalm 91:10-12). No one will labor only to have his work destroyed by catastrophe or "bring forth for calamity" (Isaiah 65:23 ASV).

A Global Center for Worship

Add to this brief overview of some of the highlights of the kingdom an incredibly beautiful religious center with all the citizens coming and going "from year to year to worship the King, the Lord of hosts" (Zechariah 14:16). This center will feature a temple of Jehovah that is described in structural detail in *eight chapters* of the prophecy of Ezekiel (Ezekiel 40-48)! Add to this the glory of the Priest-King, Jesus, and the beauty of the political capitol of the world and you can get a feel for the splendor of the kingdom rule.

Personal Rewards for Kingdom Citizens

Great personal rewards will come to kingdom citizens. They will be guests at great feasts such as the "marriage supper of the Lamb" described in Revelation 19:9. The kingdom is likened in Matthew 22 to a great feast, in Matthew 25 to a wedding, and in Matthew 26:29 to the time when Christ will once again "eat and drink" with us.

Kingdom citizens will receive the great inheritances described in the parable of the talents (Matthew 25:14-30). They will inherit the entire earth (Matthew 5:5). They will be joint heirs with Jesus himself (Romans 8:17). They will receive at least a one hundred fold return on anything that they have given up to be a disciple of Jesus Christ. This last promise is phenomenal. It is recorded in Matthew 19:28,29, where Jesus promises thrones to his twelve followers and a return "to anyone that has left houses, brothers, sisters, father, mother, wife, children or lands." The return is "one hundred times" what was given up with the added bonus of eternal life!

Eternal Stability of the Kingdom

With the average length of an earthly civilization or political empire standing at about two hundred years, it is comforting to know that the kingdom we inherit will never cease. Not only can it not cease, it can never even be disturbed or "shaken" (Hebrews 12:28). Two hundred years or two hundred billion years will fail to weaken the strength of the kingdom we have received from Jesus Christ.

VICTORY is ours! For God possesses the power and the glory forever, and we who enter the kingdom share that power and glory *with him* forever. *Victory* is ours!

12 Carrying Out the Occupation

Jesus' followers were understandably confused. After hearing their Master talk so much about the kingdom, they were sure that it was going to take place immediately. He was near Jerusalem and the ardent listeners just "knew" that at Jerusalem he was going to "make it happen." To clarify that the establishment of the kingdom was to take place in the future, Jesus told a parable. It was the parable of a nobleman who went to a distant country to have himself appointed king. Knowing that he would return after his appointment, he gave three months wages to each of ten of his servants and said to them, "Occupy till I come" (Luke 19:13 KJV).

After World War II, there were a number of defeated countries that were "occupied" by the allied forces. This was hardly a static concept. The occupation forces were charged with conducting the affairs of the vanquished nations until such a time as they could be trusted to take over their own affairs again. This is the concept that Jesus was seeking to relay in the parable of the departing nobleman. The New International Version translates the command, "Put this money to work until I come back." Jesus was obviously referring to himself as the nobleman who went away to receive appointment as king. He is away now for that purpose, and he certainly has left us with a command to engage in productive activity. He doesn't intend us just to "hang around" until he gets back!

We are the "occupation forces" of his conquest. He

secured the victory at the empty tomb and left us to conduct his affairs under the guidance of his Spirit until he returns. The world system having already been potentially conquered, he has left us to carry out the affairs of the kingdom and to "occupy" the vanquished lands. He has provided all the resources we need to complete the task and will demand accountability for the way we have invested those resources when he returns. This is our "occupation responsibility."

Whether we accept the challenge of his "occupation troops" and become productive will depend on what we do with the truths of the kingdom. An unimplemented truth has no more effect on the world than an unimplemented lie. Thus, a book full of great *truths* about the kingdom of Jesus Christ will have no positive effect whatever if the truths are not acted upon by those who hear them. They will have no more effect than a pack of great *lies* about the kingdom that never gets put into action.

I have heard it said that the world is divided into "thinker-uppers," "planner-outers" and "getter-doners." Someone else has said that the division identifies those who say, "What's happening?", those who "watch things happen" and those who "make things happen." God is the "thinker-upper" and the "planner-outer" for the kingdom. And there is a sense in which he is the "getter-doner" as well. But he has chosen to get a good bit of the kingdom work done through us! Whether he will will depend on whether we decide to *watch* the kingdom happen or help *make* it happen.

Actually, having been exposed to some kingdom truths, you may not be able to plead ignorance as an excuse for inactivity. You are *accountable* from this point forward! You now have to make a choice of your *will* on this issue. The human will is the "clutch" that links the mighty "power under the hood" with the drive train—the place where the "rubber meets the road." It will matter little that you are party to these insights of the kingdom or that you have the omnipotent Holy Spirit "under your hood". If you do not engage your *will* to transfer that supernatural horsepower to the motion of your vehicle, you will be like a car in neutral with the engine roaring—lots of power but no speed! But even if you decide to act, to get involved in the kingdom, there are cautions you must observe. There are certain extremes that you must avoid. Following are a few of them.

Fleshly Effort Vs. Pious Passivity

The first caution is against extremes of motivation, against gritting your teeth in fleshly self-effort on one hand and against lying back in pious passivity on the other. A world of evils has resulted when citizens of the kingdom have sought to take it by force in fleshly self-effort. We are warned against this in a number of places in the Scriptures. Zerubbabel was warned by a message from God through the prophet Zechariah that his leadership of Judah should not rely on "might nor power but on the Spirit of God" (Zechariah 4:6). Apart from the power of the Spirit of God, our fleshly power is worthless anyway.

Jesus observed that "from the days of John the Baptist until now the kingdom of heaven suffers violence, and the violent take it by force" (Matthew 11:12). At the trial before Pilate, Jesus again made the point that a heavenly kingdom is not to be put into effect with earthly force. He told Pilate categorically:

> My kingdom is not of this world; if my kingdom were of this world, then would my servants fight, that I should not be delivered to the Jews; but now is my kingdom not from here (John 18:36).

Jesus put this precept into practice in his responses to his accusers and attackers. At his arrest in the garden, Peter sought to carry out God's plans in human force, cutting off the ear of the high priest's servant, Malchus. Jesus commanded him to put his sword back into its sheath. He then asked permission to carry out the plans of the kingdom his own way—by reaching forward and healing his enemy's ear! In the power of the Spirit he was not overcome by evil, but he overcame evil with good. That is the "force" of the kingdom.

On the other side of this caution is the danger of becoming piously passive, relying on the "sovereignty of God" to the point that the things God chooses to do in and through us he cannot do. He can't get us off our sofas! James delivered an injunction against being "hearers" of the word and not "doers" of it. James knew that genuine faith would be translated into God-motivated action, not monastic withdrawal and self-righteous laziness.

Worldly Weapons Vs. Fleeing the Front

Another area of caution is against using the weapons of the world system to establish the kingdom. Paul gave this warning in 2 Corinthians 10:3-6. He declared that the "weapons of our warfare are not fleshly, but mighty . . . . " We don't pursue the kingdom by political log rolling, intimidation, hostile denunciations or clever manipulation of behavioral weaknesses. Those are *weak* methods. We rely on the power of the Spirit—the powerful weapon—to pull down strongholds, cast down phony rationalizations, and bring thoughts into captivity to Christ! At the same time, we don't use our reliance on spiritual weapons as an excuse to flee the military front lines. We stay in there and fight, but we "fight" with the pure heart, right motives, good deeds and love, against which no one can defend.

I remember a time when, as a college president, I tested

the effectiveness of the Spirit weapon vs. the flesh weapons. You see, I had a row among my faculty over a proposal I had made to them. There was considerable division among them as to whether this was a right course to take. It had significant consequences both to their spiritual lives and to their paychecks. I was convinced that I had sought the mind of the Lord regarding the proposal and the board of trustees had approved its enactment. But the faculty was still split.

It was annual faculty contract time and I was scheduled to have personal interviews with each faculty member. This could have provided me with a beautiful opportunity to use a few "fleshly weapons" in the "Lord's warfare!" I could make support of the proposal a condition for issuing the new contract. In the context of the contract I could more subtly "suggest" that I "really needed their support" for the new proposal. My fleshly options were numerous. I chose instead to test the kingdom method. I chose not to mention the new proposal at all in any of the faculty interviews. I chose not to use any fleshly weapons, but instead to get on my knees and ask God to bring support in the hearts of the faculty for the proposal, if indeed it was his plan. I purposed to demonstrate love and commitment even to the most vocal and aggressive opponents of the proposal.

Within a few days, all of the faculty members but two had come to me indicating that as they had prayed about the proposal and thought about it, they had come to believe that it was a good one. They wanted to assure me of their support! But what about the other two? I just thanked God that he would work in their lives in a similar manner. This was going to take more Spirit power, because these two were the most violently opposed to the plan.

Two weeks passed and one morning one of the two scheduled an appointment to tell me that God had convicted him of his wrong attitude toward the proposal, of critical remarks to others about me and the board, and of his rebellious attitude. He asked forgiveness. I granted it and we prayed together. Later in the same morning, the other of the two sought me out to communicate nearly the same words and the kingdom plan went forward with unanimous support. Obviously God could have indicated his direction and could have reguided me through a unanimous rejection of my initial notions. Nonetheless it still would have been his guidance as I operated "in the Spirit." Sometimes I wonder why I ever resort to the world's weapons. They are so ineffective!

The Personal Checklist

A maxim from management training decrees, "People do what you *in*spect, not what you *ex*pect!" Knowing this to be true, I thought I would give you an opportunity to become involved in the kingdom by presenting some of the criteria for involvement in "checklist" form. I'm even going to give you a place to put a check indicating that you have put each point into action! This first checklist is a personal one, just for you to check your availability to the King for the work of his kingdom. Don't leave one unchecked. Deal with it before you read on. This will serve as your "military preparedness inspection" as an occupation soldier in the kingdom army.

1. New Birth

Obviously one who is going to help shake the world for Jesus Christ must know him personally and must have experienced the spiritual rebirth that Jesus described in John 3:1-18. If there is a time in your life when you have acknowleged your sinfulness and have asked Christ to take your sin and give you his eternal life, you check out this one. If not, stop right here, talk to God, confessing your sin and asking his Son, Jesus Christ, to forgive you, to come into your life and give you a place in his kingdom.

I checked out on this _____

2. Cleansing and Spirit Control

The citizen of the kingdom who is effective and powerful must be completely free from any unconfessed sin and must have the Spirit of God in control of his life. If there is no wrong attitude or broken relationship, no sin that you have not confessed, then the Spirit can control and direct you. If you know of sin, confess it. If you are free from sin, ask the Holy Spirit to fill and control you.

I checked out on this _____

3. Lordship

Even if you are a citizen of the kingdom, you may still be holding on to some cherished habit, possession, desire, plan or "idol." To have the King direct you freely into kingdom victories, you must acknowledge his sovereignty over your life. If you can tell him you will go anywhere he wants you to go, do anything he wants you to do, say anything he wants you to say and give away anything he wants you to give away, he is LORD of your life.

I checked out on this _____

(NOTE: While the first checkpoint, new birth, needs to be accomplished only once, the second and third will need to be reaffirmed at any point that there is an "erosion" of the commitment. Don't hesitate to reaffirm them daily or more often if necessary. God will understand!)

The Enlistment Checklist

In addition to those spiritual decisions that make us useable in the kingdom, there are a number of other points at which, I believe, we should enlist in the cause of the kingdom. While there may be one or more of the following points in which you do not feel you can enlist, seriously consider giving your support to all of them. I'll list what I think the kingdom cause needs today. See if you can commit yourself before God to help put that point into operation in your own life or in the body of believers with which you identify. Remember, the Holy Spirit will help you!

1. **Bold Declaration of the Good News**
   The kingdom today needs to have each of its citizens boldly and openly sharing the good news of salvation through Jesus Christ in the little "world" in which he operates. Every believer must assume the accountability for sharing Jesus Christ with those with whom he comes in contact, especially those who are in his immediate and continual sphere of influence (neighbors, family, friends, co-workers, etc).
   I'll commit myself to that _____

2. **Grander Dreams and Plans**
   Every citizen of the kingdom must begin to dream grander dreams, think greater thoughts and exercise greater faith in our King. He must purpose to expand the horizons of his life and vision far beyond their present limits. He must refuse to laugh at any idea or plan God gives him because it is "too big" or "too impossible."
   I'll commit myself to that _____

3. Deeper Commitment to the Scriptures

The only guidebook we have that bears the imprimatur of our King is the Bible. The kingdom citizen must reject all attempts to explain away, water down, compromise or spiritualize the clear and simple commands of Scripture. He must commit himself to study and obey without questioning the teachings and commands of God's infallible and divinely inspired revelation.

I'll commit myself to that _____

4. Bold Recruitment of Others

There are many kingdom citizens who are not involved in kingdom affairs. We must sensitively but boldly confront them in the Spirit with a challenge to involvement. One of the greatest joys I have each year is to meet with executives of large corporations, people of great wealth and influence and leaders in the Church. I challenge them to greater sacrifice, involvement and vision for the kingdom. Making this challenge is a privilege.

I'll commit myself to that _____

5. Establishment of a Clear Strategy

If the citizen of the kingdom does not have a God-given plan, he will not accomplish much, no matter how pure his motives or how holy his life. Clear objectives and a clear plan or strategy for accomplishing them will do more to revolutionize a life for the kingdom than most people can imagine. I personally have five-year goals and plans to accomplish them. I talk over the proposed goals with God, consult with my spouse about their suitability and keep them constantly before me. This book would not have been written were it not in my five-year plan. The citizen of the kingdom who aims at nothing will achieve a direct hit. Aim at something.

I'll commit myself to that _____

6. Pursuit of Adequte Training

Just as a soldier in the military service would not presume to enter the field of battle without adequate "basic training," so the soldier in the army of the King should not presume to be effective without being trained. I am not talking necessarily about Bible college or seminary. I am talking about turning off the TV set and using some of that gained time to be taught in seminars on witnessing effectively. Above all, involvement in a body of believers where systematic, thorough study of the Word is available should be the most important aspect of training for any kingdom citizen. From correspondence courses to personal discipleship to academic degree programs, training is both available and necessary for effective kingdom service.

I'll commit myself to that _____

7. Utilization of "Secular" Discoveries

The enemy forces are constantly discovering new methods that are making their opposition to the kingdom more effective. Often the citizens of the kingdom are the last to "exploit" those breakthroughs for the cause of Christ. We must commit ourselve to the immediate and effective adaptation of such "secular" breakthroughs for the kingdom. We must trust God to enable us to utilize the discoveries without imitating the motives and objectives of the enemy.

I'll commit myself to that _____

8. A Higher Risk Offensive

For the forces of the King to be effective, they must

pursue massive offensives in the loving proclamation of the good news of the kingdom. These offensives should entail greater "risks" than ones presently being pursued. The increasingly high risk and bold offensives of the enemy leave us no choice but to launch spiritual counter-offensives that are equally "high risk" and "high visibility." Across the world the enemy forces are staging public rallies. They hold press conferences, contact people in influential positions and raise millions to pursue everything from "gay liberation" to the silencing of the Christian witness in the media. While we never can copy the motives nor use the corrupt methods, we can openly and humbly proclaim our message.

The first century Church mastered these techniques. As Jews, they went into synagogues to proclaim that Jesus was the Messiah. Hardly a low risk, low visibility strategy! As Romans, they took the message to the center of the Roman state religion and proclaimed the message in the streets. As learned believers, they took the good news of the kingdom into the intellectual centers of Athens, Alexandria and Jerusalem and into the centers of pagan religion in Corinth, Ephesus and Samaria. As kingdom messengers, we must commit ourselves, our churches, our fellowships of believers to "higher risk offensives", knowing that if we are obedient to the King, he will cover the risks!

I'll commit myself to that _____

9. Lifestyle Adjustments

The kingdom lifestyle dictates that we must make radical adjustments in the style and standard of living we pursue to advance the cause of the kingdom. I am not speaking merely of financial adjustments, although kingdom citizens in the Western world *must* make significant alterations here. I am speaking of vocational adjustments, entertainment adjustments and relationship adjustments.

Some citizens of the kingdom are "tithing their vocational careers." If they can expect to spend forty-five years in vocational careers, they are committing to give at least four-and-a-half years of vocational service working for Christ. They do this either all at once or use a few weeks or months spread throughout their careers. Many young people are committing to give at least two years to overseas volunteer work upon graduation from college or before starting a home or family.

Some kingdom citizens are choosing to live at the salary level of the missionaries they support and are channeling the rest of their income into the proclamation of the gospel. Some have chosen to give God half of all their raises for the rest of their lives. Others are increasing the percentage of their giving to the kingdom each year "so long as God enables them." Some are committing a percentage of their company's profits to the kingdom. Many are just plain refusing to get caught up in the new-car-every-year-buy-everything-in-sight mania of their consumer societies.

I know of kingdom citizens who are choosing to pursue family vacations and entertainment alternatives that will advance the cause of the kingdom. Instead of spending a vacation week fishing, they spend it at a Christian family camp. Instead of eating out at restaurants for entertainment, they are taking in an inspirational musical program. In relationship adjustments they are choosing friends that can help them grow into more effective kingdom citizens and they are "phasing out" relationships with those who are a "negative pull" on their kingdom commitments.

However the kingdom "lifestyle adjustments" affect an individual, group or family (and the Holy Spirit is the only one who can give that direction,) certain adjustments must be made. We are stewards of our resources.

I'll commit myself to that _____

10. Deeper Comradeship

One of the incredible benefits of kingdom citizenship is fellowship within the "body of the committed." Everywhere I go in the world I end up in embraces and warm, love expressions because everywhere a kingdom citizen goes, the kingdom is! I've been on my knees with other brothers and sisters of the kingdom on every continent. I've sensed the electricity of kingdom citizens praising and worshiping the King in languages that I don't even understand. I sensed the "spirit of the kingdom" even before I received the translation! I know the joy of meeting a "perfect stranger" and discovering him to be a son of the kingdom and a "precious brother" in a matter of moments.

I know what it is like to have brothers and sisters in the Spirit! I have many of them all over the world. If the kingdom is to be pursued, then we must develop a deeper comradeship among the "occupation troops." We must put an immediate and forceful end to all infighting, divisiveness, factionalism, hostility, suspicion and broken relationships. The "flow of kingdom power" goes through us to the cause only to the extent that, like the disciples at Pentecost, we are all "in one place and of one accord." The enemy laughs when we are expending valuable rounds of ammunition on our own troops!

All over the world there is a growing awareness that if we do not "hang together," then we will "hang separately." We must pledge to rely on the Spirit to give us supernatural, kingdom love for every comradein-arms of the King. We must cling tenaciously to those who are partners of the faith with us and must be peacemakers within our ranks.

I'll commit myself to that _____

I cannot emphasize the need for *kingdom love* too much. From the beginning, the force that has held together peoples of the kingdom from different social classes, racial backgrounds, national origins and political convictions has been KINGDOM LOVE. It is that love that binds us to our King. It is that love that binds us to one another. The songwriter put it this way:

> In Christ there is no East or West,
> In Him no South or North,
> But one great fellowship of love
> Throughout the whole wide earth.

● ● ●

> Join hands then, brothers of the faith,
> Whate'er your race may be,
> Who serves my Father as a son
> is surely kin to me.

● ● ●

To me, the beauty of kingdom relationships is captured in one experience I had a number of years ago outside the old wall of Jerusalem. I was leading a tour of the Holy Land and using some "free time" to get away from the responsibilities of the tour to pursue a hobby of mine. When I travel, I like to take my camera and telephoto lens to some busy marketplace or city square and hide myself away in the shadows to take portraits. Drawing in the faces of people of various origins, I record on my film the etchings of life on their faces.

While I was doing this, two teen-age boys stopped, asked in broken language about the camera and the long lens, and ooohed and aaahed over the view I gave them through the viewfinder. Suddenly, without any particular context, the one young man looked me squarely in the eye and said, "Do you love Jesus?"

I travel internationally with a little "healthy scepticism" because so many play clever angles to separate you from your American dollars. So I replied, "Why do you ask?"

"I love Jesus," he responded, "I asked Jesus in my heart."

I turned to the other young man. "Do you love Jesus?" I asked.

His face broke out in an eye, ear, nose and throat smile. "Yes!" he replied.

"Did you ask Jesus in your heart too?"

"Yes, I asked Jesus into my heart."

I couldn't restrain myself any longer. I let my smile out of its lockbox and announced, "That makes us brothers. I love Jesus. I asked Jesus into my heart too!!"

In a moment we were hugging each other right there on the streets of Jerusalem. One participant in that embrace was a Jew who had discovered Jesus as his Messiah, the King of Israel. One participant was an Arab who had found that Jesus was Allah in human flesh. One participant was a North American Gentile who had met Jesus as his personal Savior. In Jesus nothing mattered about the differences that ordinarily divide diverse people like that. We were sons of the kingdom!! The King Of kings had conquered us with his love and had brought us into his kingdom. As citizens of his kingdom we had bridges between us where once there were walls—just the way it is going to be across the whole earth someday.

The whole earth will be united in one, enormous tearful embrace when the king will take the nations of this world and make them his.

PRAY FOR IT!
TRUST FOR IT!
WORK FOR IT!
YOU ARE A CHILD OF THE KINGDOM!!